Masculinity Reforged:

Timeless Lessons for Modern Men

Darcy Carter

Ready to Go Beyond the Page?

This book will challenge you to think deeply—but real transformation happens when you take action.

To help you with that, I've created a course called **Masculinity Reforged**.

It is a guided experience with structured exercises, journaling prompts, and real-world challenges to help you apply the lessons inside this book and more.

MASCULINITY REFORGED THE COURSE

⬇️ ⬇️ ⬇️

tommy-s-school34.teachable.com/p/masculinity

TABLE OF CONTENTS

Introduction

"What does it mean to be a man?"

This question, which once had a clear answer, is now filled with confusion. Today, masculinity is viewed in two very different ways. On one side are some men who believe that masculinity means being strong, wealthy, and dominant. They believe a man's value comes from his ability to gain power and control his world. On the other side are certain progressive narratives in the media and our cultural discourse promote a softer, more emotional version of masculinity. They encourage men to be vulnerable and empathetic and question traditional gender roles.

The problem isn't with either side individually; it's that both offer incomplete views. As a result, many men are trapped between two extremes—they are expected to be both tough and vulnerable, to lead with confidence yet remain humble, to assert themselves without overshadowing others. Such mixed messages create confusion, making it hard for men to feel authentic and clear about what it truly means to be a man.

Past definitions of what it meant to be a man were much clearer. Strength, leadership, and resilience were valued. Today, those traditional ideas have weakened, leaving modern men feeling lost. *This book is not about returning to outdated stereotypes of masculinity.* Nor is it about rejecting the progress. Instead, it presents timeless masculine values while embracing the complexity of modern life. Drawing from the lives of great men throughout history, it explores how their ideas and philosophies can be used today.

This book was written to help modern men find clarity and direction in a confusing world that is filled with mixed expectations. It connects theory to real life by providing practical insights and steps that men can use in their everyday lives. Through historical lessons and modern wisdom, men will discover how to harness their inner strength, navigate emotions, and build meaningful relationships.

This book doesn't just give you vague theories or motivational speeches; it provides you with a blueprint for action. One that bridges the gap between historical wisdom and modern challenges, giving you timeless lessons from men who have shaped history. Here is just a small preview of what you will find inside:

- **Emotional Mastery**: Learn how to control your emotions without letting them control you. Drawing from historical figures who faced unimaginable pressures, you'll discover how to respond with strength, clarity, and purpose, even when life hits hard.

- **Purpose and Direction**: In a world obsessed with distractions and quick fixes, finding one's purpose isn't easy. This book will help you cut through the noise, define success on your own terms, and create a life driven by meaning rather than mindless routines.

- **Resilience in Adversity**: Life will test you. It's not a matter of if, but when. You'll gain insights from men—leaders, warriors, and visionaries—who've faced the worst. You'll learn how they stayed strong in the toughest of times.

- **Physical and Mental Discipline**: A strong mind needs a strong body. Drawing inspiration from legends like Alexander the Great and modern men who embody discipline, you'll learn how to forge habits that sharpen both your mental toughness and physical resilience.

- **Brotherhood and Relationships:** No man thrives in isolation. Inspired by the brotherhood of warriors like the Spartans, you'll understand the importance of surrounding yourself with other men who challenge and elevate you. Furthermore, you'll learn how to build loving and fulfilling relationships.

- **Legacy and Impact:** Life isn't just about what you achieve—it's about what you leave behind. You'll explore how leaders like Niccolò Machiavelli, Nelson Mandela, and others shaped history not by chasing status, but by living with purpose. You'll learn how to create a life that leaves a legacy long after you're gone.

The time has come to move beyond outdated stereotypes and oversimplified narratives. It's time for men to reclaim their strength and live with purpose! In the chapters ahead, you'll explore every dimension of what it means to be a man. Whether you're striving to become a stronger leader, forge meaningful connections, or overcome personal battles, this book is your blueprint for mastering masculinity.

Chapter 1: Evolution

—————◆◇◇◉◇◇◆—————

*"Do not pray for an easy life; pray
for the strength to endure a difficult one."*
— Bruce Lee

Masculinity Has Never Stood Still

Masculinity is not a fixed concept; it has evolved alongside history itself. Expectations of men have always depended on the time, place, and culture in which they lived. In ancient times, brute strength and warrior instincts defined manhood. Survival often depended on a man's ability to hunt, fight, and protect. As civilizations advanced, the definition of masculinity began to shift.

In the age of empires and great thinkers, traits like wisdom, diplomacy, strategic thinking, and emotional control took center stage. Men were no longer just warriors; they became philosophers, leaders, and architects of societies. In the industrial era, masculinity evolved once again. The focus shifted to discipline, hard work, and providing for one's family.

5

The modern era has brought yet another transformation. Emotional intelligence, self-awareness, and vulnerability are now part of the conversation. But while the outward expression of masculinity has evolved, certain core principles have remained constant. And to understand where we are going, we must first understand where we have been.

A Timeline of Masculinity

Ancient Masculinity: Strength, Wisdom, and Duty

In ancient times, masculinity was defined by the values and needs of each society. In Sparta, for example, being a man meant displaying strength, discipline, and loyalty. Spartan boys were taken from their families at a young age and trained rigorously to become warriors. They were taught to endure hardship, fight with courage, and prioritize the needs of their community above their own. A Spartan man earned respect through bravery in battle and an unwavering commitment to protecting his people.

In contrast, masculinity in Confucian China was very different. Rather than focusing on physical strength, wisdom, moral integrity, and self-discipline were valued. Men were expected to be virtuous leaders within their families and communities. Here, masculinity was measured not by physical dominance, but by a man's ability to lead with honor, cultivate knowledge, and maintain order in both his personal life and society.

These contrasting examples show that masculinity has never been one-size-fits-all—it has always reflected the priorities and values of the prevailing culture.

The Evolving Man: From Chivalry to the Renaissance Ideal

During the medieval period, the chivalric code defined what it meant to be a man. This code placed importance on both martial skills and moral values. Knights were expected to show courage in battle, but they also had to be humble, generous, and fair. They were judged not only by their ability to fight but by how they treated others, especially the vulnerable.

During the Renaissance, the idea of masculinity evolved to include more intellectual qualities. The ideal "Renaissance man" combined physical strength with a love for learning, showing interest in both art and science. Men of that era, such as Leonardo da Vinci, showed this mix of talent, proving that masculinity could be strong in both creative and intellectual fields.

The Industrial Age: The Emergence of the Provider Archetype

The Industrial Revolution reshaped masculinity yet again, introducing the "provider" archetype. As economies shifted and urban centers grew, men were increasingly defined by their ability to work hard, provide for their families, and maintain emotional control. The ideal man was a breadwinner, a man who was strong, dependable, and self-sacrificing. Success was measured by his ability to meet financial and societal obligations, often at the expense of personal fulfillment or emotional expression.

Modern Masculinity: Breaking the False Dichotomy

By the mid-to-late 20th century, society began to radically rethink what it meant to be a man. Feminist movements, civil rights activism, and countercultural shifts challenged the rigid expectations that had defined masculinity for centuries. Men were encouraged to embrace vulnerability, empathy, and self-expression.

Today, masculinity is more complex and varied than ever before. Globalization has merged cultural perspectives, creating a diverse range of expectations for men across different societies. In some places, traditional ideals of strength and dominance remain deeply ingrained. Meanwhile, in others, there is greater emphasis on emotional intelligence, cooperation, and adaptability. The rise of technology and social media has further amplified the confusion. While this broadening of masculinity offers men more freedom to define their identity, it has also created uncertainty.

The Modern Problem: The Trap of Binary Masculinity

Despite masculinity's historical diversity, many men today feel trapped in a rigid, oversimplified binary. Society presents them with two opposing ideals, each incomplete and unsatisfying in its own way.

The Tough Guy

This version of masculinity is based on traditional ideas about being strong, in control, and emotionally distant. It values traits like strength, control, and a "never back down" attitude. While being resilient, decisive, and self-sufficient is important, taking this idea to the extreme can lead to serious problems.

- **Isolation:** Men raised with the "man up" mentality often suppress their emotions, cutting themselves off from meaningful connections and support systems.

- **Aggression:** An overemphasis on dominance can lead to hostility, bullying, or even violence, particularly when men feel their power or status is threatened.

- **Emotional Suppression:** Internalizing pain, fear, or insecurity often manifests in mental health issues such as depression, anxiety, and substance abuse.

Men like Andrew Tate have gained popularity by promoting a tough, dominant image of masculinity, often linked to the broader "Red Pill" philosophy. This worldview emphasizes strength, control, and status as the core traits of being a man. Many lost young men have strongly resonated with it. However, it presents an unrealistic and one-dimensional view of manhood. This mindset can create unfair and rigid expectations in relationships, fostering dynamics built on control rather than mutual respect.

The Sensitive Guy

At the opposite end of the spectrum, the modern "sensitive new man" archetype champions emotional openness, vulnerability, and collaboration. It has emerged as a counter to the "tough guy" stereotype. Men are encouraged to reject outdated notions of dominance and embrace traditionally feminine qualities.

While emotional intelligence is a crucial skill for men, this model has its flaws:

- **Dismissal of Assertiveness:** Competitive drive, ambition, and decisiveness can be unfairly criticized, leaving men unsure if pursuing success makes them "toxic."

- **Overemphasis on Vulnerability:** While emotional openness is valuable, men are often left without clear guidance on how to balance it with resilience and strength. This can lead to passivity, indecision, and a lack of personal direction.

While this archetype is meant to encourage healthier masculinity, it can leave men feeling disconnected from their natural instincts.

The False Choice: Strength vs. Sensitivity

The real problem with these opposing views is that they create a false choice: be tough or be sensitive, but never be both. Such limited viewpoints ignore the fact that masculinity can adapt and depends on the situation.

Consider a father comforting his child. He demonstrates tenderness, patience, and emotional openness. Yet, that same man, when protecting his family from a real threat, will need to be strong. Neither of these roles negates the other; both are valid expressions of masculinity, shaped by the situation.

True masculinity isn't about choosing between strength and vulnerability. It's about mastering both and knowing when to apply each. The most powerful men throughout history were not one-dimensional. They were warriors and diplomats, leaders and caretakers, thinkers and fighters. The modern man's challenge is to reclaim that balance, to integrate both strength and sensitivity, dominance and compassion, ambition and humility into a masculinity that serves him rather than limits him.

Men must redefine masculinity on their terms, and that means rejecting the idea that they must be either emotionally closed off or completely submissive. Masculinity should be viewed as flexible, varied, and highly personal. To achieve this balance, men must embrace a **masculinity reforged**, one that values:

- **Strength and resilience**, but not at the expense of emotional intelligence.

- **Ambition and leadership**, without the need to dominate or diminish others.

- **Emotional openness**, while maintaining boundaries and self-respect.

- **Confidence and assertiveness**, without arrogance or aggression.

- **A deep connection to tradition**, while evolving to meet the needs of the modern world.

This isn't about pleasing society. It's about becoming the strongest, most capable version of yourself: a man who commands respect, builds meaningful relationships, and takes responsibility for his future. The days of one-dimensional masculinity are over. It's time to reforge something stronger.

Practical Exercise: Reflecting on Your Masculine Traits

Understanding your place on the spectrum of masculinity begins with reflection. By examining your strengths, recognizing areas for growth, and setting clear intentions, you can cultivate a more balanced and authentic expression of yourself.

Step 1: Identify Your Strengths

What qualities come naturally to you? Perhaps you excel at supporting and protecting those you care about. Or maybe you're a man who likes to go out there and make things happen. Recognizing your strengths is the first step in understanding how you currently embody masculinity.

Step 2: Recognize Areas for Growth

What traits do you admire in others that you'd like to develop? For instance, do you admire a friend's ability to stay calm under pressure or their talent for expressing vulnerability without fear? Identifying these areas provides a roadmap for your personal growth.

Step 3: Set an Intention

Choose one trait you want to cultivate and think about how you can practice it in your daily life. For example:

- If you want to build resilience, commit to taking on a small challenge this week— for example, dealing with a difficult task you've been avoiding.

- If you want to embrace vulnerability, have an honest conversation with someone you trust about how you're feeling.

Step 4: Check In with Yourself

Growth doesn't happen overnight. Reflect regularly on how these efforts are shaping your life. Are they helping you build stronger relationships, achieve your goals, or feel more aligned with your values?

The Freedom to Define Masculinity

Breaking free from the binary definitions of masculinity is both liberating and transformative. When you stop trying to fit into a predefined mold, you create space for authentic growth and deeper connections. You give yourself the chance to be strong when needed, compassionate when appropriate, and everything else in between.

This journey takes courage. Not the kind you see in action movies, but the quiet strength required to be your true self. By accepting the complexity of masculinity, you can let go of expectations and embrace a version of manhood that is uniquely yours.

In the end, what defines a man isn't how well he fits into society's expectations, but how honestly he lives his truth. Masculinity isn't a final goal; it's a journey of discovering who you are. Every small step you take is progress toward becoming the man you are meant to be.

Chapter 2: Purpose

——————— ✦◇◇◉◇◇✦ ———————

"There is no failure except failure to serve one's purpose."
— Henry Ford

The Power of Purpose

In the late 12th century, Mongolia was a place of constant fighting, where competing tribes battled for power and survival. Among these tribes was a young boy named Temüjin. Born into a weak clan, he was left behind by his allies after his father was killed. At just 10 years old, he experienced betrayal, captivity, and exile. All alone in the tough wilderness without his family, he felt hopeless.

But Temüjin didn't accept his fate. Despite his youth and the overwhelming odds against him, he held onto one thing that many others lacked: a clear sense of purpose. While others focused on survival, he looked at the bigger picture. He wanted to unite Mongolia and end the cycle of warfare, which seemed like an impossible goal. Yet the path to achieving it was anything but smooth. He was captured and made a slave by a rival clan, forced to live in chains while his enemies tried to break him.

Each failure could have ruined Temüjin, but he kept on going. He was determined to unite the Mongol tribes under his leadership. When most men would have given up, his purpose kept him moving forward. Through his relentless drive and strategic brilliance, he began to achieve what no one had before: he united the warring tribes of Mongolia. Slowly, his scattered alliances grew into an unstoppable force. Tribes that had fought for years came together, united by a common goal that went beyond their differences.

When Temüjin finally realized his vision, he wasn't just a boy seeking survival—he had transformed into Genghis Khan, the "Universal Ruler." His strong leadership and clear goals helped him build the largest empire in history, which stretched from the Pacific Ocean to Eastern Europe.

Genghis Khan's rise wasn't about being born into privilege or having superior resources. His story shows how powerful having a purpose can be for a man. It helped him endure tough times and overcome challenges that would have defeated most people. What made his purpose so powerful wasn't just its scale. It was its clarity. He knew exactly what he wanted, and that vision guided his every action toward achieving his goal.

The Modern Problem: A Life Without Purpose

Today's challenges may differ from those our ancestors faced, but that doesn't mean that the need for a man to have a purpose is any less essential. A lack of purpose can be harmful, and is an issue for modern men, who feel lost in a world of constant noise.

Why am I doing this?

The digital age has amplified this struggle. With every notification, social media post, and news alert, we're pulled in countless directions. Hours pass by as we mindlessly consume content, making us feel emptier and more disconnected than ever. Meanwhile, we feel like something important is missing.

When you don't have a clear sense of purpose, life can feel like you're:

- **Waking up without direction:** Days blend together, filled with pointless tasks. Activities turn into simple checkboxes instead of steps toward a bigger goal.

- **Living someone else's dream:** When you don't follow your own path, you end up helping someone else's vision.

- **Falling prey to distractions:** Social media, video games, and endless entertainment provide an easy escape. They fill the hours but leave you feeling drained and unfulfilled.

Lack of direction doesn't mean you're lazy or unmotivated. It's a sign that you're spinning your wheels and you have no traction. The human mind craves meaning, and when we don't find it, we tend to fill the gap with busyness, distractions, or fleeting pleasures.

People often assume that money, status, or the latest toys will make us happy. But real happiness comes from what matters to us personally. Without a clear purpose, you're left adrift, chasing goals that don't resonate with who you truly are. You might spend years climbing a ladder, only to realize it was leaning against the wrong wall.

Purpose Doesn't Have to be Grand, Just Clear

One of the greatest misconceptions about purpose is that it needs to be epic or world-changing. It's false beliefs such as this that keep many men stuck,

MASCULINITY REFORGED

waiting for inspiration to reveal their destiny. But the truth is, purpose doesn't need to be epic—it just needs to be clear and deeply personal.

Genghis Khan didn't begin with a vision to conquer half the world. His purpose was simpler: unite his people and secure their survival. It was specific, actionable, and meaningful to him.

Your purpose doesn't have to make headlines or impress anyone else. It only needs to:

Resonate with your values: Purpose isn't about what society tells you is important. It's about what feels important to you.

Give you direction: A clear purpose acts as a filter, helping you prioritize what matters and discard what doesn't.

Inspire consistent action: Purpose isn't static. It's something you work toward every day.

How to Find Your Purpose

Finding your purpose requires figuring out what is important to you. But this won't happen by itself; you really have to think about it and try new things. In the process, you will start to discover what really matters to you. And if you feel lost or uncertain about your purpose, that's okay. Purpose isn't

21

static; it evolves as you grow and learn. What's important is starting the process. Here's how:

Step 1: Reflect on What Matters Most

Begin by asking yourself questions to uncover what truly resonates with you:

1. **What Are My Core Values?**

    o   What principles do I want to live by? For example, do you want to live a life that embodies loyalty, integrity, creativity, service, and growth?
    o   Values act as the foundation for your purpose, ensuring it aligns with who you are at your core.

2. **What Brings Me Joy and Fulfillment?**

    o   Think about the activities that give you a deep sense of satisfaction, the ones that make you lose track of time.
    o   Fulfillment often comes from actions that challenge you, engage your strengths, and connect you to others.

3. **Who Do I Want to Impact?**

    o   Consider the people, communities, or causes that you feel drawn to help.

o   Purpose is often rooted in service. How
    can your skills or passions benefit
    others?

4. **What Do I Want to Leave Behind?**

o   Envision your legacy. How do you want
    to be remembered by family, friends,
    and the world?
o   Purpose often comes from the desire to
    create something lasting and meaningful.

5. **What Challenges Am I Willing to
   Endure?**

o   Purpose isn't necessarily about what
    makes you happy, but what you're
    willing to struggle for.
o   What are the goals or causes you're
    willing to sacrifice for?

Step 2: Experiment and Take Action

Clarity comes through action, not overthinking.
Start small by exploring different paths:

- Volunteer for a cause you care about.
- Take a class or workshop to develop a skill
  that excites you.

- Set a short-term goal aligned with your interests, such as completing a project or joining a group.

Each step will help you refine your understanding of what feels meaningful.

Step 3: Define Your Mission Statement

Once you've reflected on what matters most to you, write your thoughts into a personal mission statement. It should be a clear, actionable expression of your purpose. Written out, it will serve as your compass, guiding your decisions and reminding you what you're working toward.

How to Write Your Mission Statement

1. **Focus on What Truly Matters to You**

   o Consider your values, passions, and long-term goals.
   o What excites you? What challenges are you motivated to tackle?

2. **Be Specific and Actionable**

   o Avoid vague phrases like "I want to be successful" or "I want to help people." Instead, define what success or helping others looks like for you.

For example, "I want to build a sustainable business that empowers local artisans and supports my family."

3. **Emphasize the Impact You Want to Make**

   o Who or what do you want your actions to benefit?
   o Think about how your efforts will ripple outward, creating positive change.

Examples of Mission Statements

- **For Family**: "I strive to be a present and loving father who inspires my children to pursue their dreams and face challenges with courage."

- **For Personal Growth**: "My purpose is to constantly learn and grow so I can lead a life of creativity, integrity, and service to others."

- **For Career**: "I aim to build a business that provides financial freedom for my family and opportunities for my employees to thrive."

- **For Community**: "I want to mentor young men in my community, helping them build confidence, resilience, and a sense of purpose."

Revisit and revise your purpose statement over time. It isn't set in stone. As you grow, your experiences and priorities will evolve. Thus, your mission statement should evolve with them. Make it a habit to revisit your purpose regularly. Check in monthly, yearly, or whenever you feel stuck, and adjust as needed.

Reframing Purpose for the Modern World

Your purpose may not seem impressive to others, and that's okay. True fulfillment comes from living in a way that matters to you. Some men find their purpose in being great fathers and husbands. Others find it in mastering a skill. There is no single definition, only this truth: your purpose must matter to you.

Purpose is the foundation of a meaningful life. It's a compass, keeping you focused on what truly matters and steering you away from distractions. Without it, men drift—chasing superficial achievements, wasting time on meaningless pursuits, and wondering why they feel unfulfilled. A man without purpose is a man without direction.

Purpose isn't something you stumble upon. It's built through reflection, action, and persistence. You don't need ideal conditions to start. Look at Genghis Khan—he wasn't born into power, but he carved a path with sheer determination. You don't need permission, wealth, or perfect circumstances. You need purpose.

Life will test you. It will challenge your beliefs, shake your confidence, and demand that you prove your resolve. Without purpose, these challenges will break you. With purpose, they will forge you into something stronger.

Chapter 3: Discipline

"Discipline equals freedom."
— Jocko Willink

Mastering Life, One Battle at a Time

Before Jocko Willink became famous for his strong discipline and leadership, he was an ordinary kid. There were no signs that he would become a decorated Navy SEAL officer, bestselling author, and mentor to many. He didn't grow up with any privileges or extraordinary advantages. What made him different was something simpler but more powerful: a strong work ethic and a willingness to face discomfort.

As a young man, Jocko was drawn to challenge and structure, finding purpose in the disciplined environment of the military. His journey was tough, and he quickly realized that success in the SEAL teams didn't come from natural talent or luck. It came from hard work, determination, and a commitment to being the best. The SEAL training, called BUD/S, aimed to break men down and push them beyond their limits. Many men chose to quit, but Jocko thrived in the chaos. Discipline was the essential element he used to overcome any challenge.

Once deployed, Jocko's discipline was no longer just about personal growth. It became a matter of survival. During the Iraq War, he led one of the most highly decorated special operations units of the conflict. As a leader, he demanded nothing from his team that he didn't demand from himself first. In the heat of combat, his team didn't just follow him because of his rank—they followed him because they trusted him and knew that his discipline meant he was always prepared.

After retiring from the military, Jocko maintained his strong work ethic. He became a popular leadership coach, helping top executives and organizations worldwide apply the ideas of extreme ownership and discipline. He wrote books, started a successful podcast, and created a fitness brand, all while sticking to the habits that had helped him in the military.

For Jocko, discipline is freedom in every aspect of life. Freedom isn't about doing whatever you want, whenever you want. It's about eliminating the unnecessary decisions that slow you down. When you wake up at the same time every day, when you commit to a fitness routine, when you structure your work with precision,you free yourself from distractions, indecision, and wasted time. The paradox is simple: by creating structure, you gain freedom: freedom from chaos, procrastination, and weakness.

The Modern Problem: A World Without Discipline

Discipline isn't just for soldiers or elite athletes. It's a tool that anyone can use to take control of their lives. However, many men struggle to develop even a small amount of discipline, something that has become less common in a world that values convenience and instant gratification. Once seen as a key part of being a man, it's now often viewed as limiting or old-fashioned.

Modern life offers endless opportunities to avoid discomfort. We have access to food, entertainment, and more at our fingertips. As a result, people now expect quick success instead of putting in the effort that it used to take. We are conditioned to think that if goals don't happen quickly, they're not worth pursuing. The desire for instant rewards has weakened our ability to stick to long-term goals and to bounce back from setbacks.

The consequences of this shift are evident in every aspect of men's lives. Without discipline, their physical health deteriorates as they opt for convenience over consistency. They find it hard to focus, and they are affected emotionally as the lack of discipline manifests as avoidance. Instead of facing challenges head-on, men turn to distractions to escape their problems.

Ultimately, life becomes a series of missed opportunities and unrealized potential. Goals are abandoned not because they're unattainable, but because the effort required to achieve them feels overwhelming. Relationships suffer, careers stagnate, and self-respect diminishes. As a result, many men find themselves wondering why they feel unfulfilled and directionless.

Discipline doesn't involve perfection or punishment, but rather taking ownership. Choosing to do what needs to be done, even when it's difficult or inconvenient. It's about building habits that align with long-term goals rather than short-term gratification. When men embrace discipline, they reclaim control over their lives, refocusing their energy on what truly matters and creating momentum toward success.

Jocko's message—"Discipline equals freedom"—is more relevant now than ever. In a world filled with distractions, discipline provides clarity. In a culture of comfort, discipline builds resilience. And in a time where many feel lost, it offers a roadmap to purpose and fulfillment.

Building the Framework for Success

Discipline is the act of choosing long-term growth over short-term comfort, and it's in these daily choices that character and strength are forged. Every time you resist the temptation to skip a workout, hit snooze, or procrastinate, you're not just building a bad habit—you're shaping your identity. Discipline reinforces your ability to rely on yourself, and over time, it becomes second nature. When you consistently push yourself beyond your comfort zone, you grow stronger. This strength doesn't mean never failing; it means learning to get back up every time you do.

Here are some key areas to build discipline in:

Morning Routines

Jocko Willink's 4:30 AM wake-up habit is iconic. While not everyone needs to rise before dawn, committing to a consistent morning routine can have a powerful impact. A disciplined morning routine provides structure and momentum, laying the groundwork for success. Your routine could include:

- **Journaling**: Reflect on your goals, express gratitude, or process your thoughts. This will give you mental clarity that can set a positive tone for the day.

- **Exercise**: Moving your body first thing in the morning energizes you, boosts dopamine, and reinforces the habit of prioritizing your health.

- **Meditation or Prayer**: Cultivating mindfulness or connecting with your spiritual side helps you approach the day with focus and calm.

- **Planning the Day**: Identify your top priorities and set clear intentions, ensuring that you act with purpose rather than reacting to distractions.

Again, the key to this isn't the time you wake up, but the commitment to start your day intentionally. Whether you're an early riser or a night owl, a structured morning routine anchors your discipline and ensures that you hit the ground running.

Physical Training: Building Discipline Through Movement

Discipline in fitness goes far beyond achieving a certain look. It's about creating a body that supports your ambitions and builds discipline in every aspect of life. Regular physical training teaches you to embrace discomfort, push through limits, and build confidence. It can be done in a number of ways:

- **Strength Training:** Lifting weights challenges your body and mind, teaching you to focus on gradual improvement.

- **Cardiovascular Work:** Running, cycling, or swimming improves endurance and mental toughness, showing you the value of persistence.

- **Martial Arts or Team Sports:** Activities that involve skill-building and camaraderie can enhance both discipline and a sense of community.

The discipline gained through physical training spills over into other areas of life. Commitment to show up at the gym, run that extra mile, or push through one more set builds the mental toughness required to tackle life's broader challenges.

Ownership of Actions: The Foundation of Discipline

It means accepting complete responsibility for your life, including your successes, failures, and everything in between. This mindset eliminates excuses and empowers you to take action.

- **Successes**: Celebrate your achievements but recognize that they came from your effort and decisions.

- **Failures**: Instead of blaming others or external circumstances, ask yourself: What could I have done differently? How can I improve next time?

- **Daily Choices**: Discipline means recognizing that every small decision—what you eat, how you spend your time, and how you respond to setbacks—shapes your life.

Ownership isn't just about accountability; it's about empowerment. When you take responsibility for your actions, you reclaim control over your future.

Practical Steps to Build Discipline

MASCULINITY REFORGED

1. Start Small, But Start Daily

Discipline doesn't require radical, overnight changes. Begin with something simple but significant. For example, make your bed every morning, drink water first thing, or commit to five minutes of meditation. These small habits compound over time, creating a solid foundation for larger goals.

2. Track Your Progress

Use a journal, app, or checklist to track your habits. Tracking your progress reinforces your efforts and builds momentum. It also provides valuable insights into patterns and areas for improvement.

3. Embrace Discomfort

Discipline means leaning into discomfort, whether it's resisting the urge to sleep in, sticking to a challenging workout, or staying focused on a tedious task. Discomfort is temporary, but the growth it produces is lasting. Lean into it.

4. Create Accountability

Tell a trusted friend or mentor about your goals and ask them to check on your progress. Joining a group with shared interests, like a fitness class or

36

mastermind group, can provide additional accountability and encouragement.

5. A Simple Starting Point

Commit to one small act of discipline today and stick with it for a week. Examples include:

- **Cold Showers:** A solid way to start your day with a challenge that builds mental toughness and wakes you up.

- **Daily Exercise:** Even ten minutes of movement reinforces the habit of prioritizing health.

- **Journaling:** Write down one goal or reflection each day to build mental clarity.

At the end of the week, take a moment to reflect on how this habit impacted your mindset, energy, and confidence. Small steps pave the way for monumental changes.

Discipline Equals Freedom

Discipline concerns power, not rigidity or self-punishment. Power over weakness. Power over distraction. Power over the version of yourself that settles for less. Every act of discipline is a vote for the man you want to become. It sharpens your resilience, strengthens your resolve, and gives you the ability to face life head-on.

But more than that, discipline is freedom. The freedom to control your time instead of being controlled by impulses. The freedom to pursue excellence without being weighed down by excuses. The freedom to act with intention rather than being a slave to circumstance.

Jocko Willink's life proves that talent, luck, or waiting for the right moment aren't essential for a man's success. What a man truly needs to do is show up, do the work, and embrace discomfort until discipline becomes second nature. It's the edge that separates men who achieve greatness from those who make excuses.

Discipline won't make life easier, but when you master it, you don't just master your schedule, your habits, or your goals—you master yourself. And through that mastery, you gain the greatest freedom of all: the ability to live life on your own terms.

Chapter 4: Resilience

—— ◆◇◇◎◇◇◆ ——

"Success is not final, failure is not fatal:
it is the courage to continue that counts."
— Sir Winston Churchill

The Resilience of Winston Churchill

When Winston Churchill became Prime Minister in 1940, Britain stood on the edge of destruction. Nazi Germany had already steamrolled through Europe, crushing France, Belgium, and the Netherlands in a matter of weeks. The once-mighty British Army had barely escaped annihilation at Dunkirk, retreating home battered and demoralized.

The skies above London roared with the sound of Luftwaffe bombers, which unleashed relentless waves of destruction. Entire neighborhoods were reduced to rubble, and civilians lived in constant fear of the next air raid. At sea, German U-boats prowled the Atlantic, sinking supply ships and choking Britain's vital lifelines. Without food, weapons, and reinforcements, Britain risked being starved into submission. Many believed defeat was inevitable. The United States remained hesitant to intervene. Britain was alone, outgunned, and on the brink. This was the moment Churchill stepped forward.

Churchill became a leader when many doubted him. His past was marked by controversial decisions and political missteps, including the disastrous Gallipoli campaign during World War I. As a result, he spent years in political exile, where he was ignored and dismissed as a relic of the past. Many doubted he could bring the country together for the tough times ahead. Yet he was not a man to shrink from adversity.

When Britain needed help the most, Churchill was ready to lead. As the bombs rained down on London during the Blitz, he refused to hide in a bunker or retreat to the safety of the countryside. Instead, he walked among the ruins, standing shoulder to shoulder with the people he led. He listened to their fears, shared their grief, and inspired them to believe that victory was possible. And he didn't deny the dangers they faced or sugarcoat the reality of war. Instead, he embraced the enormity of the challenge and inspired others to rise to it. His speeches, delivered with conviction, became lifelines for a nation on the brink:

"We shall fight on the landing grounds. We shall fight in the fields, and in the streets, we shall fight in the hills. We shall never surrender!"

By the end of World War II, Churchill's leadership had become synonymous with resilience itself. He had weathered criticism, overcome monumental failures, and inspired an entire nation to stand firm in the face of overwhelming adversity. His life shows us that we can overcome challenges even in the toughest of times. Not just by using strength, but by staying resilient and never giving up.

The Modern Problem: A Culture of Giving Up Too Soon

While the world may not be experiencing war on the same scale as World War II, resilience is just as critical today as it was then. Many men struggle to push through adversity, not because challenges are any greater than before, but because society has conditioned them to see hardship as a signal to stop rather than as an opportunity to grow.

Modern culture often frames struggle as a sign that something is wrong, that if something is difficult, it must not be meant for you. Such a mindset creates a dangerous habit: avoidance over perseverance. Instead of embracing difficulty as a necessary part of progress, many men retreat at the first sign of discomfort. The result? A generation unable to handle setbacks, searching for shortcuts instead of solutions.

Our modern world values instant gratification. Social media constantly presents us with highlight reels. We see entrepreneurs celebrated for their billion-dollar companies, athletes for their championship wins, artists for their masterpieces. But rarely do we hear about the countless setbacks and sacrifices they endured along the way. The emphasis is always on the final achievement, not the journey that made it possible.

In addition, technology has conditioned us to expect immediate results in almost every aspect of life. With one-click shopping, same-day deliveries, and instant access to information, we have become used to getting what we want on demand. Such convenience makes it harder to embrace the slower, more challenging processes required for real growth and lasting success. Whether we're learning a new skill, building a career, or improving our health, we become frustrated when we don't get immediate results.

Patience and perseverance can feel outdated, almost unnecessary. When success doesn't happen quickly, it's easy to believe it never will. The modern expectation that life should be smooth and effortless makes even minor setbacks feel overwhelming, causing many of us to give up too soon. Without the ability to embrace struggle and persist through difficulties, real achievement becomes harder to attain. Each time you walk away from a difficult situation, you reinforce a pattern of avoidance that makes it even harder to push through future obstacles. The more you quit, the more you train your mind to see quitting as the easier option. Over time, this can create a fear of failure, making it even harder for you to take risks or to step outside of your comfort zone.

"Every challenge presents a chance to grow, but avoiding them amounts to missed opportunities, leading to a life of missed potential. Dreams and ambitions remain just that—dreams—never realized because the hard work required to achieve them was abandoned too early. Progress requires persistence, and without it, life can become a cycle of unrealized goals and untapped potential.

Perhaps the most painful cost of giving up too soon is the frustration and regret that follows. The thought of what could have been often haunts people far more than failure ever could. Failure or regret, you choose. Failure, at least, provides valuable lessons. But giving up without fully trying leaves behind a nagging sense of "what if," a persistent feeling that you didn't give yourself the chance to succeed.

While the temptation to quit may seem like the easy way out, the long-term consequences can have a worrying impact. Pushing through challenges, even when they seem impossible, is what builds true resilience and opens the door to a fulfilling, meaningful life.

Resilience is Forged in Everyday Choices

Winston Churchill's life shows us that resilience isn't about grand gestures or superhuman strength, but about consistent, small acts of persistence. Every time you choose to move forward despite setbacks, you reinforce your ability to handle adversity. Resilience is forged in everyday choices. It's waking up early to work on a goal when it's easier to stay in bed. It's returning to a project after criticism instead of quitting. It's swallowing your pride to apologize rather than letting anger win. Such small decisions, repeated over time, create momentum and build a resilient mindset.

Churchill embodied this principle. Under the constant pressure of war, he inspired a nation through his daily acts of leadership, even when defeat seemed likely. His resilience wasn't about moments of glory, but the unglamorous grind, the discipline to show up, and the courage to persist. Success, whether in leadership, sports, or business, rarely comes from a single defining moment. It's the product of relentless effort and sacrifices made without applause. Achievements celebrated publicly are just the visible peaks of long and unseen journeys.

Practical Steps to Build Resilience

Churchill didn't win the war in a day. He focused on one battle, one alliance, one decision at a time. Similarly, your challenges can be conquered through steady, consistent action. Your accomplishments may seem minor at first, but eventually they will form the foundation of a resilient mindset.

Here are some actionable steps you can take to build resilience:

1. **Reframe Setbacks**
   o How to Practice: When something goes wrong, ask yourself: *"What can I learn from this experience?"*
   Example: If a presentation at work falls

flat, view it as an opportunity to improve your communication skills.

2. Break Challenges Into Small Steps

o How to Practice: Focus on the next small action you can take, rather than being overwhelmed by the entire challenge.
Example: If you're overwhelmed by a big project, start by outlining just the first task.

3. Develop a "Next Time" Mindset

o How to Practice: Instead of dwelling on mistakes, focus on what you'll do differently in the future.
Example: After an argument, reflect on how you could handle a similar situation better next time.

4. Surround Yourself With Support

o How to Practice: Build a network of people who encourage, challenge, and uplift you.
Example: Share your goals with a trusted friend who can hold you accountable and remind you of your potential during tough times.

The Transformative Power of Resilience

Resilience will transform you into a different kind of man, one who can face adversity without the fear of being undone by it. Challenges will no longer feel like barriers; they will become opportunities to prove your strength. Every time you reframe a setback, take a small step forward, or refuse to give up, you'll be building the foundation of a resilient mindset. Over time, this mindset will transform your relationship with adversity, allowing you to approach life's challenges with confidence, courage, and clarity.

Resilience isn't a gift reserved for the lucky or the naturally strong. It's the courage to continue, no matter what life throws your way. It's a skill you develop by showing up, day after day. Churchill's greatest victories weren't the result of sheer luck or overwhelming power. They were the result of his commitment to keep going, even when success seemed impossible.

Success is never final, and failure is never fatal.

Hey!

If you want to go beyond reading and actually apply what's in this book, I've created a full online course called Masculinity Reforged.

You can join it here:

tommy-s-school34.teachable.com/p/masculinity

Chapter 5: Emotions

———————◆◇◇◉◇◇◆———————

*"Between stimulus and response, there is a space.
In that space is our power to choose our response."*
— Viktor Frankl

Strength Amid Chaos

In 165 AD, the Roman Empire was at its peak. It covered a vast area, had powerful armies, and influenced many cultures. However, an invisible threat was spreading. A deadly disease known as the Antonine Plague swept through the empire. Soldiers, farmers, and senators all became ill. The plague didn't spare even the richest aristocrats in their marble villas nor the poorest citizens in crowded streets. Entire towns were reduced to ruins within weeks. Crops withered in the fields as sickness claimed the lives of those who worked the land. Trade, once the lifeblood of the empire, ground to a halt as fear spread faster than the disease itself. Enemy tribes at the borders of the empire saw weakness. Once a strong and orderly empire, Rome was now on the verge of collapse.

At the center of the storm stood the Emperor, Marcus Aurelius. Each day, he received reports of soldiers falling ill, provinces rising in revolt, and cities descending into panic. Many leaders in his position might have given in to the immense pressure. But instead, he remained calm and composed. While fear and chaos spread throughout his empire, he focused on what he could control: his thoughts, his actions, and his leadership. He didn't spend his evenings feeling sorry for himself or seeking pleasure. Instead, he reflected quietly on his thoughts. Alone with his thoughts, he wrote in his private journal, what would later become known as *Meditations*—reminding himself of the Stoic principles that had guided him throughout his life.

One principle, above all, stood out to him during this crisis:

"You cannot control what happens around you. You can only control how you respond."

Marcus Aurelius didn't give in to hopelessness or act out in frustration. He controlled his emotions and remained clear-headed. Emotional control helped him to lead with wisdom and compassion. Throughout his life, he remained calm in the face of chaos and became a source of stability for the entire empire. Through his actions, he proved that a man's strength isn't in controlling the uncontrollable, but in mastering himself. Even today, his words serve as a reminder of how important it is to control your emotions, especially when faced with difficult situations.

The Modern Plague: Emotional Struggles in a Chaotic World

Today, men aren't fighting a literal plague, but many are grappling with a modern version—anger, anxiety, depression, and emotional instability. We live in an era where the pressure to succeed and to project an image of perfection is constant. Society's expectations, fueled by the constant presence of social media, make failures and setbacks seem bigger than they really are.

At work, men find themselves buried under mounting deadlines and constant demands. Stress builds up slowly, sometimes unnoticed, until even minor setbacks hit hard, chipping away at a man's confidence and leaving him questioning his competence and self-worth. In turn, the workplace becomes not just a place of professional challenge, but an emotional battleground.

In relationships, misunderstandings, unresolved conflicts, and subtle criticisms can drive partners apart. Men are taught to hide their feelings, seeing vulnerability as a sign of weakness. Sadly, this leads to emotional suppression, causing feelings of isolation and resentment, even with close partners. Failure to express emotions creates a barrier and turns a support system into another area of silent struggle.

Then there's social media, with its overwhelming influence on our lives. With each scroll, you're confronted with images of exotic vacations, career successes, perfect bodies, and ideal families. Seeing these idealized images of life can cause feelings of inadequacy and self-doubt. You may feel that no matter what you achieve, it's never enough.

In this environment, emotional struggles are easy to overlook or dismiss. But beneath the surface, they're silently shaping how men see themselves and define their worth. Many react in pacifying ways that only make their problems worse. One typical response is lashing out in anger, which often acts as a shield, hiding deeper emotions like fear, sadness, or feelings of failure. Such emotions can be hard to face or express. So they stay hidden, leading to ongoing frustration and regret. Over time, unchecked anger pushes people away, leaving men alone and misunderstood.

Alternatively, some men respond by shutting down completely. Rather than addressing their emotions head-on, they bottle them up in an attempt to "push through." However, suppressed emotions have a way of surfacing in unhealthy ways—withdrawing from loved ones, avoiding responsibilities, or gradually drifting into destructive coping mechanisms. What starts as an effort to remain strong can manifest in excessive drinking, addictive behaviors, or a reliance on distractions to numb the discomfort. Yet the longer these emotions remain unaddressed, the more they compound, creating a vicious cycle that becomes harder to break.

Emotional control—recognizing your emotions, pausing before speaking, and choosing your response—offers a breakthrough.Many men might misunderstand what this means and think it means hiding their feelings. True emotional control involves understanding your emotions and choosing how you respond, rather than denying them. Hiding your feelings only keeps them buried for a while before they come back to haunt you.

Think of your emotions like the weather. You can't stop the rain from falling or the wind from blowing, but you can choose how to prepare for the storm. Emotional control means noticing how you feel and choosing how to react. Yes, you will feel angry, anxious, and frustrated. That's all part of being human. No matter how disciplined you are, life will challenge you. But experiencing these emotions doesn't mean you have to act on them immediately. There's a critical space—a pause—between feeling an emotion and choosing your response. That space is where your true power lies.

Emotions are signals, not commands. Anger may indicate that a boundary has been crossed. Anxiety could be a sign to prepare for an upcoming challenge. These emotions are important and deserve attention, but they don't require impulsive reactions. Recognizing this distinction is the key to mastering emotional control.

Imagine Marcus Aurelius facing the pressure of ruling an empire during a deadly plague. When anger or fear crept in, he didn't suppress those emotions. Instead, he paused, examined them, and asked himself constructive questions before responding. Pausing allowed him to make decisions from a place of strength, not weakness. The Stoics referred to this practice as *prohairesis*, a Greek term meaning the ability to pause, think, and act according to reason rather than impulse. For Marcus Aurelius, this idea was not just a theory; it was something he practiced every day.

Train your emotions

Emotional control is a mental muscle you build. The more you train it, the stronger it gets. Like any muscle, it requires consistent effort and intentional practice. Without emotional control, you will be like a ship without a rudder, pushed around by whatever emotion you feel. With emotional control, you can guide your life in whatever direction you want, no matter what happens around you.

Here's how you can train your emotional muscles:

- **Start Small:** Notice your feelings in challenging situations. For example, if someone cuts you off in traffic, take a moment to pause before you react.

- **Identify the Trigger:** Ask yourself, *"Why do I feel this way?"* Knowing where your emotions come from helps you respond in a thoughtful way.

- **Reframe the Situation:** Instead of saying, "This is unfair," try, "This is an opportunity to practice patience."

Mastering emotional control doesn't mean you'll never feel anger, anxiety, or negative emotions again. You'll be able to face them without being ruled by them and will still be able to feel the "good" emotions. With the knowledge learned in this chapter, you will have the power to respond. Marcus Aurelius faced challenges that could have crushed even the strongest leaders. Remaining composed amid chaos set him apart, and it's a lesson that resonates just as strongly today.

Now, you don't need to be an emperor to practice mental mastery. You can control your thoughts and reactions in everyday life, especially in everyday moments that you might overlook. For example, think about your daily commute. It can be frustrating when you encounter traffic jams, delays, or unpredictable drivers. While these situations are out of your control, your response to them is not. Instead of feeling angry or stressed, you can choose to change your perspective. Use the time in traffic to listen to an audiobook. Or to reflect on your day calmly, or practice gratitude for having a car, or a job. By changing how you think about your commute, you will develop mental strength.

Social media is another place where you can grow your emotional control. It's easy to get caught up in the non-stop flow of perfect images and to feel jealous or insecure when you see others' perfect lives. Instead of comparing yourself, take a moment to think about why you feel this way. What does it reveal about your goals and desires? Taking this moment, even if it's brief, helps you shift your focus from comparison to self-improvement. Rather than letting others' success affect how you see yourself, you can use it as a sign to work on your own growth.

Criticism can happen at work, in relationships, or even from strangers online. The natural response is to become defensive. However, instead of reacting defensively, take a deep breath and approach criticism with curiosity. Think of it as a chance to grow. Is there any truth in this feedback? Can it help me improve my skills or see things I might have missed? By reflecting instead of reacting, you will find opportunities for growth.

In moments of crisis, people don't look to the loudest person in the room; they look to the calmest. Staying calm when things are falling apart builds confidence and trust. It turns you into a source of stability for your family, friends, colleagues, and yourself.

The Transformative Power of Choice

The Stoics believed that every moment presents a choice: to let the world dictate your emotions or to reclaim your power by focusing on what you can control. Each time you make the choice to respond with clarity rather than impulse, you strengthen the foundation of your character. You become the kind of man who is unshaken by storms, one who is guided by reason and purpose instead of fleeting emotions.

The world will always be unpredictable. Problems will arise, challenges will test you, and emotions will shift. But real strength has never been about controlling the outside world, but about mastering how you respond to it.

Chapter 6: Courage

———————— ◆◇◇◉◇◇◆ ————————

"When you grow up in comfort, that will produce a very balanced and a good person. But it will not create the hunger to be the best in the world.

— Arnold Schwarzenegger

The Greatest

In 1967, Muhammad Ali was at the top of his boxing career as the heavyweight champion of the world. He was a global icon. A man who had captivated the world with his speed, power, and unmatched confidence. He had it all: fame, fortune, and the aura of a man who knew he was the best. But when the U.S. government drafted him to serve in the Vietnam War, he was faced with a decision that would test his strength far beyond the boxing ring. Ali refused to go. Standing before the world, he declared:

"I ain't got no quarrel with them Viet Cong."

He was fully aware of what his refusal would cost him, and yet, he didn't flinch. The consequences came swiftly. He was stripped of his title, banned from boxing during his prime years, and vilified by the media. He went from being celebrated as a national treasure to being branded a traitor. He also faced financial ruin, lost his boxing license, and was sentenced to five years in prison, though he remained free while appealing his conviction.

Ali could have taken the easy way out. He could have stepped into line, served quietly, and resumed his career without disruption. Instead, he stood firm in the storm and refused to betray his beliefs, knowing full well the price he would pay. For nearly four years, he was kept from the sport he had dominated. But even in exile, his spirit remained unshaken. Time proved him right. In 1971, the Supreme Court overturned his conviction, and Ali returned to the ring, reclaiming his status as a champion. But by then, his legacy was far greater than boxing. He was no longer just an athlete—he was a symbol of courage.

Don't Be a Pussy

When you're young, there's always that one moment that sticks with you, the moment when you either stand your ground or back down. Maybe it was facing a bully in school, speaking up when something didn't sit right, or standing tall when it felt easier to run. Those moments define us, and whether we realize it or not, they shape who we become.

Courage is often misunderstood as simply being fearless or physically strong, but it's much more than that. True courage is about standing firm in the face of adversity, making difficult decisions, and taking action even when fear is present. It's not about eliminating fear; it's about having the courage to move forward despite it.

In modern masculinity, courage takes many forms, whether it's standing up for your beliefs like Ali, pushing through personal hardships, or taking responsibility for your life when it's easier to blame others. The challenges men face today may not always be public battles against an entire government, but they can be just as demanding — like standing up to toxic relationships, pursuing dreams, or breaking free from societal expectations.

Courage takes many forms in everyday life, and each type plays a crucial role in shaping who we are. Physical courage is the most visible form, pushing past limitations in health, fitness, and endurance. It's the willingness to challenge your body, whether it's committing to a grueling fitness routine, recovering from an injury, or simply stepping into discomfort. And it isn't just about brute strength;

it's about persistence—choosing to keep going even when the journey is tough.

Emotional courage, on the other hand, operates on a deeper level. It's the ability to face vulnerability, rejection, and emotional hardships head-on. It's admitting your fears, opening up about insecurities, and seeking help when needed. All of it requires immense courage. Yet, many men avoid this kind of courage because they fear that vulnerability means weakness. However, the truth is that emotional courage allows for authentic connections, self-growth, and inner peace. It's the foundation for building meaningful relationships and for developing a strong sense of self-worth.

Then there's moral courage, which involves standing up for what you believe in, even when it's unpopular or inconvenient, speaking the truth in difficult situations, holding yourself accountable to your values, and defending what is right in the face of opposition. It's easy to stay silent or compromise, but moral courage demands that you act in alignment with your principles, regardless of the consequences. It's the kind of courage that shapes great leaders and creates lasting change.

Finally, social courage is about taking risks in relationships, career, and personal ambitions. It's the courage to put yourself out there, to pursue dreams that others might doubt, and to face the fear of failure in pursuit of something greater— whether it's changing careers, approaching someone you admire, or stepping into new social environments. Ultimately it's about embracing the unknown and going beyond your comfort zone, bringing growth and new connections as you move toward the life you truly desire.

Each of these forms of courage is interconnected, reinforcing one another in the pursuit of a fulfilling life. Whether it's physical, emotional, moral, or social, true courage is about showing up and taking action—no matter how difficult that may seem.

Building Courage

Understanding how the brain processes fear is crucial to developing courage. Fear is a natural response to uncertainty and perceived threats. It triggers the fight-or-flight response, leading many to avoid challenging situations. However, courage doesn't simply concern eliminating fear, but learning how to manage it.

When we face and overcome our fears, we build the courage to tackle bigger challenges. Whether it's public speaking, confronting personal failures, or taking risks in relationships, each act of courage creates a foundation for greater strength.

Here are a few exercises to build courage daily:

1. **The Fear Exposure Challenge:** This week, pick one thing you've been avoiding due to fear and take one step toward facing it.

2. **Daily Acts of Courage:** Commit to doing one thing every day that challenges your comfort zone—whether it's having a difficult conversation or trying something new.

3. **Courage Journaling:** Write down your fears, the actions you took to face them, and what you learned from the experience.

Commit to a Life of Courage

Courage isn't something you tap into once and forget about. It's a lifelong commitment, a muscle that strengthens with use. Neglecting it is a step backward. Practicing it strengthens your willingness to stand up, face the unknown, and keep moving forward, even when the odds are stacked against you.

Muhammad Ali's story reminds us that courage isn't just about standing in a ring and throwing punches. It's about standing firm in your beliefs, even when the world turns against you. It's about refusing to let fear dictate your choices, knowing that true strength isn't found in comfort but in challenge.

Every man will face moments where he must choose—step up or back down, speak the truth or stay silent, push forward or retreat. The difference between those who carve out meaningful, fulfilling lives and those who merely exist is simple: the courage to act.

There is no perfect moment to be courageous. The time is now. Take a risk. Speak your mind. Face the challenge you've been avoiding. Start today, because the man you become is built in the moments where you choose to act despite fear. One courageous step today could change the course of your life. The only question is, will you take it?

Chapter 7: Humility

◆◇◇◉◇◇◆

*"The best way to find yourself is
to lose yourself in the service of others."*
— Mahatma Gandhi

The Power of Knowing You Don't Know It All

Humility? That's like being caught with your pants down, right? It feels weak, like you're admitting defeat or letting someone else take control. Humility doesn't mean putting yourself down. Humility is having the strength to recognize that you don't have all the answers. It's owning your limitations and constantly working to improve. It's the difference between the guy who thinks he knows it all and the one who actually does.

Without humility, you stop growing because you ignore valuable feedback. You end up being the guy who's too proud to ask for help. Meanwhile, everyone else gets ahead. So, before you write humility off as some soft, passive virtue, think again. Humility separates the men who pretend they've got it all figured out from the ones who actually do. Real strength isn't just about being tough; it's also about being smart enough to know when you need to step back and listen.

How Gandhi Used Humility to Defeat an Empire

Few people in history have demonstrated humility like Mahatma Gandhi. Born in 1869 in British-controlled India, he grew up witnessing the harsh realities of colonial rule. His people were treated as second-class citizens in their own land. Naturally, this could have filled him with anger and resentment, but instead, he chose a different path—one of humility. He realized that true strength did not come from fighting back with violence, but from standing firm in the face of injustice without losing dignity.

Gandhi was a humble man. When the ruling British treated people unfairly, he didn't get angry. Instead of hate, he tried to show them what was right. When he was in jail or when he was hurt, he stayed calm. Through kindness and patience, he inspired people to stand up for what was right without using violence. Ultimately, his commitment to nonviolence and self-restraint led to India's independence. Furthermore, he left a legacy that continues to influence movements for justice worldwide.

Gandhi's story teaches us that you don't have to be weak or passive to be humble. He showed us that humility is having the strength to stay true to your values even when the world tries to break you. He demonstrated that power can also come from being humble.

The Power of Humility in Personal Growth

The moment you think you've got it all figured out is the moment you stop growing. A humble man accepts that he doesn't have all the answers and that there is always more to learn. Such a mindset helps him to approach challenges with a sense of curiosity rather than defensiveness. It allows him to learn from his mistakes without letting them define him. Additionally, it encourages continuous progress rather than complacency.

The most successful men aren't the ones who assume they're the smartest in the room. They're the ones who stay teachable, seek advice, and remain open to growth. Humility keeps their ambitions sharp and egos in check because they know that no matter how much you achieve, you can never stop getting better.

A man who embraces humility understands that every challenge is an opportunity to sharpen himself. Instead of getting defensive or making excuses, he asks, *"What can I learn from this?"* His mindset separates those who keep rising from those who get stuck.

Ego is The Biggest Obstacle to Humility

The ego thrives on comparison and it is the biggest obstacle to humility. The ego drives us to seek validation, to prove our worth, and to avoid admitting mistakes. Naturally, this makes it difficult to embrace humility without feeling weak. However, true strength lies in the ability to control your ego rather than letting it control you.

Being more humble requires you to realize when your ego is in the way. This can happen when you are defensive in an argument, feel the need to be right all the time, or hesitate to ask for help. By becoming more self-aware, you can break down your ego and develop a more humble mindset. Of course, this requires effort and practice.

Some actionable ways to cultivate more humility include:

1. **Practice active listening:** Focus on understanding others instead of just waiting for your turn to speak.

2. **Express gratitude daily:** Acknowledging the contributions of others reinforces humility and appreciation.

3. **Admit mistakes openly:** Taking responsibility for your actions builds integrity and self-respect.

4. **Learn from everyone:** Approach each interaction with the mindset that everyone has something valuable to teach you.

5. **Engage in self-reflection:** Regularly assess your actions and motivations to ensure they align with your values.

Humility in the Modern World

In today's world, where social media rewards loud voices and self-promotion, humility is more important—and more difficult—than ever. The pressure to seek validation, to constantly showcase success, can make it tempting to chase applause instead of real achievement. But the truth is, true confidence doesn't need to be bragged about. Strong men don't waste time proving themselves to others; they let their actions speak for them.

"Humility doesn't mean diminishing yourself or downplaying your successes; it means recognizing that growth never stops, wisdom comes from listening as much as leading, and respect is earned through your actions—not your bragging. Men who have the greatest impact are those who lift others up and who remain open to learning.

Gandhi's life proves that humility is a choice, a discipline, and a strength. It requires self-awareness, restraint, and the ability to rise above ego. The men who embrace it don't just gain respect—they create lasting influence. Because, in the end, success isn't measured by what you take, but by what you give.

Chapter 8: Kindness

"Being nice and being kind are not the same thing. Nice people say what you WANT to hear. Kind people say what you NEED to hear.

— Steven Bartlett

The Overlooked Strength

Okay, kindness... really? That doesn't sound very masculine. Why are we even talking about this? That's the reaction a lot of men have when kindness is brought up in discussions about masculinity. We're told that men should be strong and dominant. But the thing is, true masculinity isn't defined by being hard for the sake of it; it lies in having strength and choosing to use it wisely.

I recently attended a friend's wedding, and what he did for his guests was next-level. He didn't just send out invites and expect people to figure things out. He took care of everything. Travel, hotels, a luxury boat trip, and even the suits we wore. No one had to stress about logistics or costs. Some might look at that and say, "That's just being generous," or "He is buying favors," but I saw it differently. He was showing leadership through kindness. He set the tone for the experience, made sure people felt valued, and created an incredible atmosphere.

Men are often raised to be independent and competitive. And while there's value in all of that, it's led to a culture where kindness is seen as a liability. We've been conditioned to believe that if you're too kind, people will walk all over you. That if you help others too much, you're being taken advantage of. That if you show too much care, you're soft. These ideas have created an environment where men hesitate to be kind, fearing it will cost them respect. But true strength isn't about acting tough—it's about knowing when to be tough and when to be kind.

There's a reason people say, "Nice guys finish last." In many cases, they do. But that's because being "nice" and being kind aren't the same thing. A "nice" man is often a people-pleaser. He is someone who bends over backward to avoid conflict, who says yes when he really means no, and who prioritizes keeping the peace over standing firm in his values. Niceness is often rooted in fear— the fear of rejection, of disapproval, of not being liked. It's a passive approach, an attempt to gain validation by sacrificing personal boundaries.

Kindness, on the other hand, is intentional. It's not rolling over to please others, but choosing generosity while maintaining self-respect. A kind man doesn't give because he's afraid to say no. He gives because he has something real to offer. He leads with strength, not submission. His kindness isn't a plea for approval; it's a reflection of his confidence and capability. A kind man is abundant. He isn't kind because he has to be. He's kind because he can afford to be. He's built himself into someone who doesn't need to manipulate or seek approval to feel valued. He has the resources, the strength, and the self-respect to take care of himself and still lift others up. His kindness comes from power, not weakness.

Think about the men you respect the most. Are they the ones who treat others like crap? Are they stingy? Or are they the ones who uplift, mentor, and support others while still standing firm in their power?

Andrew Carnegie, The Ruthless Giver

Andrew Carnegie was, by all accounts, a savage businessman. He built his empire in the steel industry with a ruthless drive, outmaneuvering competitors and amassing a huge fortune in the process. He wasn't soft, nor was he passive. He played the game of capitalism as aggressively as anyone ever had. And yet, by the end of his life, he would give away nearly ninety percent of his wealth, believing that a man who died rich had failed his moral duty.

Carnegie's story is one of transformation. He was born into a poor Scottish family and immigrated to America in search of a better life. From a young age, he worked tirelessly, climbing his way up from a factory worker to becoming one of the wealthiest men in history. He understood struggle, and that understanding shaped his views on power and responsibility. He knew what it meant to be on the bottom, and when he reached the top, he didn't forget.

Carnegie's philosophy of kindness stemmed from empowerment as opposed to blind generosity. He didn't believe in just handing people money—he believed in giving them the tools to succeed. That's why he dedicated his fortune to building over 2,500 public libraries, founding universities, and funding social programs that provided education and opportunity. Ultimately, he showed that a man can be both aggressive and kind.

The Practical Strength of Kindness

Kindness isn't just a moral virtue—it's a strategic advantage. Being kind while staying strong sets respected people apart from those who are forgotten. This is true in friendships, business, and leadership. People remember how they were treated. When a man operates from a place of both power and kindness, he becomes someone others want to be around.

In relationships and friendships, kindness builds loyalty. A man who consistently shows up, supports, and gives without hidden motives builds more meaningful connections. In business, kindness is often the hidden force behind success. People want to work with, and for someone they respect and trust. No one is drawn to a man who is stingy with his money, his time, or his willingness to help others. A man who withholds out of fear or insecurity signals weakness, not strength.

Don't be a stingy man. But don't be a pushover, either. The difference between kindness and being a pushover is knowing when to be kind and when to stand firm. Kindness doesn't mean tolerating disrespect, letting people take advantage of you, or saying yes to everything. It means being kind on your terms while also having the backbone to say no when necessary.

Here's how to practice strength through kindness:

- **No stinginess**: A strong man gives freely and generously. He doesn't hold back out of fear of scarcity.

- **Don't keep score:** Give because it's who you are, not because you expect a return. Generosity is an extension of power, not a transaction.

- **Set boundaries:** Give freely, but only to those who appreciate it. Don't waste your energy on people who only take.

- **Walk away from disrespect**: If someone abuses your kindness, remove them from your life.

- **Be firm in your decisions:** Saying no is a form of strength. Don't be afraid to turn people down.

- **Lead by example**: Show kindness not because you seek approval, but because it aligns with your values.

- **Recognize manipulation:** If someone is only nice when they need something, don't reward them. Give your time and support to those who would do the same for you.

A strong man is generous without expectation— not because he seeks approval or personal gain, but because generosity aligns with his values. He gives because that's what strong men do. The moment kindness becomes transactional, it loses its power. In contrast, a weak man serves not out of true generosity, but as a means to seek validation or manipulate others into giving something in return.

The mistake most men make is believing that kindness means endless availability. It doesn't. Kindness without boundaries leads to exhaustion, resentment, and being taken for granted. Strength without kindness creates isolation. The key is balance. A man must be able to say no. He must be willing to walk away from those who exploit his generosity. If someone mistakes kindness for weakness, that's their misunderstanding—not his failing. True kindness is given freely, but never at the cost of self-respect.

The men who master this balance are those who lead with kindness while commanding respect. They give, but they do not bend to manipulation. They help, but they do not enable. They uplift, but they do not tolerate disrespect. Strong men say no out of kindness because they mean it, while weak men say yes out of niceness because they don't.

Small acts of kindness have a ripple effect that extends far beyond what we see. The right word at the right time can change someone's life. A single act of generosity can set off a chain of events that alters the course of another person's future. The strongest men understand that power is not just about domination—it's about the mark they leave on the world.

Chapter 9: Honesty

———————— ✦◇◇◉◇◇✦ ————————

"The foundation of all virtues is truth."
— Confucius

You're a Liar

We all tell lies at some point. Sometimes, we tell small lies to avoid conflict or to protect our image. Other times, we lie to ourselves to stay comfortable. Dishonesty creeps into our lives in more ways than we care to admit. But the truth is, every lie, no matter how small, weakens you.

Honesty, on the other hand, is the foundation of real strength. It's not about brutal truth for the sake of it. No, it's about living in a way that aligns your words, actions, and values. Being honest isn't always easy because it requires confronting difficult realities, even when lying seems like the easy path. But the reward is a life lived without fear. A life without the burden of maintaining appearances, and without the regret that comes from betraying yourself.

A man's word should be as solid as his actions. When you speak, people should believe you. Not because you demand it, but because you've proven yourself to be honest. In business, relationships, and friendships, honesty is what separates men of substance from those who crumble under scrutiny. A reputation for honesty builds trust, while dishonesty, even in small doses, leads to doubt, broken relationships, and lost respect.

The Viking Code of Truth

Throughout history, those who stood by their word built the strongest communities, alliances, and legacies. Nowhere was this more evident than in Viking society. While often remembered for their raids and battles, the Vikings built their world on loyalty, honor, and truth. A man's word was everything. Dishonesty wasn't just frowned upon. It could cost a man his reputation or even his life.

The Viking code of honor, known as *drengskapr*, placed a high value on honesty. To be considered a true warrior, one had to commit to one's promises. The strength of a man's word was just as important as the strength of his sword. Oaths were sacred, and breaking them was one of the greatest disgraces a man could suffer. Deception and dishonesty were seen as signs of cowardice and weakness. Those who spoke and lived with truth earned the respect of their peers and the gods alike.

Despite the passage of time, the Viking way serves as a powerful lesson for modern men: the world will always test your word. A man who speaks his truth, stands by his commitments, and refuses to trade his honor earns something far greater than wealth or status. He earns the trust of those around him. And in the end, a legacy built on truth is the only one that stands the test of time.

Sam Harris and the Modern Perspective on Honesty

While we no longer live in a time where a broken oath could lead to exile or death, dishonesty still carries heavy consequences. Lies—both big and small—erode trust, create stress, and weaken our relationships. The struggle for truth remains as relevant now as it was in Viking times, but in the modern era, it manifests in different ways.

In his book *Lying*, Sam Harris explores the psychological and social cost of dishonesty, arguing that even the smallest lies carry far-reaching consequences. While we often justify small deceptions as harmless or even necessary, Harris suggests that even little lies can create big problems for us. When we lie, we feel stressed because we have to remember our lies and worry about getting caught out. Harris suggests that being completely honest (always telling the truth) can help us feel more free and less worried.

A man who tells the truth doesn't waste energy remembering lies or maneuvering around contradictions. He gains trust effortlessly because his words and actions are consistent. As a result, he builds real relationships, free from the shallow foundations built on half-truths and manipulation.

In the end, honesty isn't about following a rigid moral code—it's about freedom. A man who lives by the truth carries no weight of deception, fears no exposure, and earns respect through his integrity. He stands taller, moves with certainty, and ultimately surpasses the man who relies on lies.

Practical Exercises to Cultivate Honesty

Practicing honesty in your life requires consistent effort and reflection. Honesty is more than telling the truth, it's developing strength. The more you practice honesty, the more natural and effortless it becomes. Here are some simple exercises to help you be more truthful in your daily life:

1. Radical Honesty Challenge (One-Day Practice)

For one full day, commit to being completely honest in all of your interactions. This doesn't mean being harsh or insensitive. You want to express yourself truthfully with emotional intelligence and tact.Notice where you are tempted to exaggerate, omit details, or tell small "white lies." Instead, choose honesty. At the end of the day, journal about your experience. Did it feel liberating or challenging? What situations tested your commitment to honesty the most?

2. The Viking Oath Exercise

Inspired by the Vikings' strong commitment to their word, write down an oath or promise to yourself regarding an area of your life that requires more honesty. For example, it could be related to fitness, relationships, or a personal goal.

Example: "I vow to be honest with myself about my health habits and take responsibility for my fitness."

Revisit this oath weekly and hold yourself accountable for living by it.

Speak your Truth

Despite its clear benefits, practicing honesty doesn't come without challenges. Many of us struggle with honesty because they fear confrontation and potential consequences. Admitting a mistake at work, sharing true feelings in a relationship, or facing difficult truths about ourselves can feel overwhelming. Concerns about rejection, criticism, or damaging our reputation often lead us to choose silence or tell half-truths instead.

Another challenge is balancing honesty with tact and empathy. Brutal honesty can sometimes harm relationships rather than strengthen them. Therefore, it's important to deliver the truth in a way that's constructive rather than hurtful. Doing so requires emotional intelligence and the ability to consider the feelings of others while remaining truthful.

Ultimately, the long-term benefits of honesty far outweigh the temporary discomfort lying may bring. Living truthfully fosters deeper relationships, increases self-respect, and builds a sense of confidence and freedom that cannot be achieved through lies.

In a world full of lies, being honest is a bold choice. A man who speaks the truth, even when it's difficult, commands respect. People know he won't say something unless he means it. In turn, his relationships are stronger, his reputation unbreakable, and his conscience free from the burdens of deception.

So the choice is yours. Keep bending the truth, hiding behind small lies and fake smiles, or step into a life where your word is strong and believable. Choose honesty, and it will build a legacy that no lie can destroy.

Hey!

If you want to go beyond reading and actually apply what's in this book, I've created a full online course called Masculinity Reforged.

You can join it here:

tommy-s-school34.teachable.com/p/masculinity

Chapter 10: Love

"Love is the beauty of the soul."
—Saint Augustine

Incels and Misogynists

Love and sex are two of the most misunderstood and misrepresented aspects of a man's life. From locker room talk to online fantasies, men are bombarded with conflicting messages: Be the dominant alpha. Show empathy. Suppress your emotions. Chase success, and women will follow. But real love and fulfilling relationships require more than just status and attraction. They demand self-awareness, emotional intelligence, and the ability to connect on a deeper level.

Some men approach love and sex like an all-you-can-eat buffet—sampling whatever looks good at the moment without considering the long-term consequences. They chase casual encounters only to find themselves feeling empty and craving something more. At the other end of the spectrum, millions of men aren't even at the buffet. Loneliness among men is one of the unspoken crises of modern masculinity. Many feel invisible, disconnected, and unsure of how to navigate relationships. They watch others feast while they starve.

In response to this confusion, men have sought refuge in movements like the Red Pill and MGTOW (Men Going Their Own Way). The Red Pill community frames modern relationships as a power struggle. It emphasizes dominance, hypergamy, and the idea that men must prioritize status and self-improvement above emotional connection. Some ideas in this mindset, like self-reliance, ambition, and caution in relationships, can be useful. However, an extreme version of this thinking leads to a distrust of women, which can turn relationships into a game of power instead of a chance for real connection.

On the other hand, MGTOW takes a different approach: stepping away from relationships completely. Many men feel disillusioned by modern dating and see relationships as losing options. Instead, they choose to focus on personal freedom, careers, and self-sufficiency. While it's wise to prioritize self-improvement and avoid harmful relationships, withdrawing completely has its downsides. By avoiding relationships, men miss out on the deep connections and meaning that healthy love can provide.

At their core, both movements are reactions to the real frustrations men face. Men influenced by these movements react by either trying to control women or avoiding them entirely. Yet neither extreme leads to fulfillment.

The Cautionary Tale of Napoleon and Josephine

Napoleon Bonaparte was a brilliant military leader who rose from humble beginnings and became the Emperor of France. He built an empire, led armies, and influenced the fate of nations. However, despite his skills in war and leadership, his personal life was full of emotional ups and downs. Josephine, the woman he loved, became one of the biggest distractions and disappointments in his life.

When Napoleon met Josephine, she was a widow with a reputation in Parisian high society. Older than him and experienced in the art of charm and seduction, she captivated him completely. While Napoleon was fiercely devoted, Josephine was far less committed in the beginning. She had affairs and didn't match his feelings, making him desperate for her attention. His love letters to her were filled with passion, obsession, and insecurity—something out of character for a man who was dominant in every other aspect of his life. His obsession with her became a weakness.

As Napoleon's power and influence grew, their relationship dynamic shifted. Josephine, once indifferent, became more devoted, but Napoleon had grown disillusioned by then. Her infidelities and initial emotional distance had left deep scars. Despite his continued love for her, he began to pull away. Eventually, he made the painful decision to divorce her—not because he no longer loved her, but because she could not provide him with an heir. Although in his final exile on the island of Saint Helena, after losing his empire, he kept a locket with her portrait inside. She remained, in many ways, the one battle he had never truly won.

Napoleon and Josephine's relationship serves as a strong warning about love, power, and masculine identity. Napoleon's obsession with Josephine made him emotionally unstable in a way no battlefield ever could. His power and status as the ruler of Europe didn't guarantee loyalty or devotion. Despite his brilliance as a strategist, he allowed his emotions to cloud his judgment.

When a man places a woman at the center of his universe without balance, he risks losing his sense of self. While men should fight for meaningful relationships, they must also recognize when a dynamic is unhealthy and have the courage to walk away.

The Masculine Role in Love: Leadership Without Control

Napoleon's story illustrates what happens when a man allows obsession to override his sense of self. Love should enhance a man's purpose, not consume it. True masculinity in relationships isn't about control, nor is it about being passive. It's about leading with presence, strength, and emotional intelligence.

A man in a healthy relationship doesn't demand submission or constantly seek approval. Instead, he provides stability, direction, and trust. In doing so he creates an environment where love flourishes. A masculine presence in love is built on these key foundations:

- **Emotional Stability:** A woman looks for security in a relationship. This can be threatened by a man who is emotionally reactive or insecure. Being strong in love means being reliable and calm. Emotional stability involves controlling one's feelings and creating a safe space for a partner to share hers.

- **Clarity and Direction:** A man must have a vision for his life, and his relationship should align with that vision. Without clear direction, a relationship drifts and becomes uncertain. This means knowing where you're headed and ensuring your woman feels safe in that journey.

- **Communication and Trust:** A strong man doesn't avoid difficult conversations. He communicates openly and listens intently. Love is handling conflict with patience and wisdom, and not avoiding it. Trust is built through clear, honest, and consistent communication, and not through silence. A man must be able to express his needs, set boundaries, and, most importantly, listen without defensiveness when his woman shares her feelings.

- **Presence:** Presence is more than just physical availability; it's also about emotional engagement. That means being attentive, responding with care, and showing up when it matters most. A woman doesn't just want a man who is physically there—she wants a man who is truly with her. This means putting your phone down, making eye contact, and actively engaging in conversations. A man who prioritizes presence makes his woman feel loved.

- **Love:** Love isn't just a feeling; it's a choice you make daily. It is not about grand gestures or dramatic expressions of passion; it's about consistency, effort, and showing up in ways that matter. It can be found in the little things—remembering details that are important to her, supporting her dreams, and making her feel safe, understood, and valued.

- **Respect and Admiration:** Love without respect eventually fades. A woman wants to admire her man—to look at him with pride, knowing he is strong, reliable, and worthy of her trust. Respect is built through character, discipline, and how a man carries himself. It's in the way he treats others, the way he upholds his values, and the way he approaches life. If a man loses self-respect, he loses the respect of his woman. And when respect is gone, love leaves.

- **Protection and Provision:** - A man must protect his woman—not just physically, but emotionally and mentally. Protection means standing up for her, ensuring she feels safe, and shielding her from unnecessary stress or harm. It also means providing not just financial support, but stability, guidance, and emotional strength. A woman wants to know that her man can handle life's challenges and that he will always have her back.

- **Commitment and Reliability:** A woman needs to know that she can count on her man. This isn't just about monogamy; it's about being a man of your word. If you say you'll do something, do it. If you make a promise, keep it. Flakiness, inconsistency, and a lack of dependability kill trust.

- **Emotional Leadership:** A man must be the emotional anchor in his relationship. Women are naturally more emotionally expressive, and they look to their man for stability. A man who remains calm in chaos, who reassures instead of reacting, and who provides emotional guidance creates a relationship dynamic built on trust, stability, and security.

Ultimately, being masculine in a relationship means creating a space where both partners can grow. A strong relationship is built on trust, respect, and emotional safety. With a strong foundation, the relationship is more likely to withstand the challenges that life inevitably brings.

Sex and the Masculine Mindset

Just as men can approach love in a way that weakens or strengthens them, they can approach sex the same way. Many men grow up believing that their worth is tied to sexual conquest. More partners validate the man's ego. But this is flawed thinking, and will lead only to emptiness and an insatiable hunger for more. A man must ask himself: Am I chasing sex for validation, or am I pursuing intimacy that truly enriches my life? Sex should not be an escape or a tool for validation. It should be an extension of a deeper emotional connection. Sex, when approached with depth and purpose, becomes a source of connection and fulfillment instead of a temporary thrill. A masculine approach to sex means understanding its deeper significance.

Here are some ways to improve your sex life:

- **Treat Sex as a Bonding Experience:** When combined with trust and connection, sex becomes a strong emotional anchor, reinforcing the bond between man and woman.

- **Prioritize Quality Over Quantity:** Meaningless encounters may provide temporary pleasure, but they often lead to emotional emptiness. A man who prioritizes quality over quantity finds deeper satisfaction.

- **Project Confidence:** Confidence in the bedroom isn't only about dominance or performance; it's also about understanding desires, communicating openly, and respecting boundaries.

- **Build Anticipation:** Sexual attraction doesn't begin in the bedroom. It starts with the way you interact daily. A man who builds tension through flirting, teasing, and small gestures of affection throughout the day cultivates deeper desire. Passion fades when sex becomes routine or expected. Anticipation keeps the spark alive.

- **Cultivate Passion:** - Maintaining passion in a relationship requires continuous exploration and growth together. It means staying physically, emotionally, and intellectually engaged with your partner rather than falling into complacency.

Adventure and spontaneity should remain a priority. That can be through shared new experiences, open conversations about desires, or simply making time to connect on a deeper level.

- **Introduce Variety:** A fulfilling sex life requires growth, creativity, and effort. If a man allows his relationship to become stagnant, boredom sets in, and attraction fades. And that's not because monogamy is limiting, but because he stopped trying. True variety isn't about changing partners (unless that's your preference); it's about constantly rediscovering and evolving with the one you choose. A man who leads in this area constantly finds new ways to increase excitement.

- **Prioritize and Health:** Sexual performance and satisfaction are deeply tied to overall health. A man who neglects his body will feel it in the bedroom. Optimal testosterone levels, stamina, and confidence all stem from taking care of oneself. A strong, energetic, and self-assured man naturally enhances the sexual connection he shares with his woman.

- **Provide Emotional Aftercare and Connection:** What happens after sex is just as important as what happens during it. A man who values connection understands that intimacy extends beyond the physical act—whether it's through affectionate touch, meaningful conversation, or simply holding his partner. Small moments like these deepen the bond between man and woman.

Sex thrives when both partners actively contribute to keeping the spark alive. Understanding and cultivating sexual polarity—the dynamic balance between masculine and feminine energy—ensures that desire remains strong. When partners intentionally nurture their differences, it creates a strong dynamic between them. In turn, this helps to strengthen both emotional and physical closeness over time.

The Buffets of Life: Choose What Feeds You

In love and sex, as in life, men must make a choice. Some indulge mindlessly, consuming everything placed in front of them with no thought for the consequences. Others starve themselves, resigning to isolation, convinced that connection is impossible. Neither path leads to fulfillment. The key is learning how to choose wisely.

For the man lost in fleeting encounters, the lesson is clear: Depth matters more than numbers. Chasing endless options doesn't fill the void—it widens it. Love and sex are at their most powerful when they serve as extensions of meaning and connection. Not as distractions or ways to validate ego.

For the man struggling with loneliness, the challenge is different but equally important. Avoidance isn't the answer. If you are invisible in the world of relationships, the solution isn't withdrawal—it's growth. Strengthen yourself, sharpen your social awareness, and step forward. Women aren't the enemy, nor are they the key to your worth.

The man who understands the deeper significance of love and intimacy doesn't stumble through life waiting for things to happen. He builds himself, his relationships, and his future. He doesn't chase endlessly, nor does he hide. He makes deliberate choices that align with his purpose and values.

So, ask yourself: Are you looking for a quick fix, or are you ready to pursue something real?

Chapter 11: Brotherhood

—————— ✦ ◇◇◉◇◇ ✦ ——————

*"I got love for my brothers but we can never
go nowhere unless we share with each other."*
— Tupac Shakur

The Band of Brothers

A man alone can be strong, but a man with brothers is unbreakable. There is a reason why history remembers the greatest warriors, leaders, and men not as individuals, but as part of a brotherhood. The Spartans at Thermopylae, the samurai clans of Japan, the men of Easy Company in World War II—each was forged in battle, but their true strength came from their loyalty to one another.

Brotherhood is more than friendship. It is trust, loyalty, and knowing that the man beside you would fight for you as you would for him. It is built in struggle, hardened in adversity, and proven in moments of fire. Easy Company, the 506th Parachute Infantry Regiment, 101st Airborne Division (the men known as the Band of Brothers), lived and died by this code. On D-Day, June 6,

1944, they parachuted into enemy territory under heavy anti-aircraft fire. Scattered, disoriented, and cut off from their units, they regrouped not out of duty, but out of a deep bond that had been forged long before the battlefield.

At the Battle of the Bulge in December 1944 came their greatest test. Surrounded by German forces in one of the coldest winters on record, they were cut off from reinforcements, lacking food, medical supplies, and winter gear. The enemy bombarded them relentlessly, demanding their surrender. But they refused. Through resilience and an unbreakable will, they held the line, playing a pivotal role in halting Hitler's last major offensive. It was the final chapter in a campaign defined by courage, sacrifice, and loyalty. Their war was over, but their bond remained unbreakable. Medals, promotions, or personal glory weren't their goals—they fought for the man beside them.

Isolation in the Digital Age

Today, many men struggle alone. As they grow older, the natural social bonds that once came effortlessly through school, sports, or shared experiences begin to fade. Work responsibilities, family obligations, and personal ambitions often take priority, leaving them little time or energy to maintain deep friendships. As a result, many men end up with acquaintances rather than true friends.

Adding to the challenge is the absence of strong male mentorship in modern society. In the past, men had guidance from fathers, uncles, and community leaders. Today, with the breakdown of traditional community structures, many young men grow up without guidance. Left without mentors, they often turn to online influencers who offer advice that is generic, impersonal, or plain bad. Additionally, it fails to provide the genuine connection that comes from real-life relationships.

Men without a supportive network are more likely to face mental health issues as they struggle alone. Beyond the mental and emotional consequences, isolation can have serious effects on physical health. Studies have shown that chronic loneliness can be as damaging as smoking fifteen cigarettes a day, increasing the risk of heart disease, stroke, and premature death. The human need for connection is not just psychological—it is biological. Neglecting it can have devastating effects on overall well-being.

Humans are social creatures by nature, and men thrive in environments where they feel supported. The Band of Brothers understood this truth deeply. Together, they were better. Like them, you too need a tribe—a group of like-minded men who will hold you accountable, push you to grow, and stand by you in times of need.

Building Your Brotherhood

Building friendships in the modern world requires effort and intent. It begins with reaching out and taking the time to invest in friendships. Whether it's reconnecting with an old friend, seeking a mentor, or joining a community. Maybe being social feels overwhelming. But it doesn't require grand, sweeping gestures. All you need are some simple and consistent actions.

Step One: Reconnect With What You've Lost

Think about your friends from the past. The ones you laughed with, leaned on, and made plans with. Many of those friendships likely faded because life got in the way. Work, family, and responsibilities quietly pulled you apart. Rebuilding those connections starts with a single act: reaching out. It could be as simple as sending a text, making a call, or meeting for a coffee. Yes, it might feel awkward at first, but most people appreciate being remembered, and they will welcome the opportunity to reconnect. The key is to make the effort and show that you care about them.

Take five minutes right now to reach out to a friend. Send a text, make a call, or message them online. Suggest a specific time to catch up, such as grabbing coffee or going for a walk.

Example messages:

- "Hey, it's been a while. Want to grab coffee this week and catch up?"
- "I was thinking about you today. Let me know when you're free to hang out!"
- "Want to hit the gym together sometime this week? Could use a workout partner!"

The simple act of reaching out can be the first step in rebuilding or strengthening your brotherhood.

Step Two: Share Experiences

New connections are easily formed through shared activities. Humans bond through shared experiences, and doing something together creates a foundation for deeper friendships. Think about the things you love or the skills you want to learn. Whether it's joining a gym, attending a martial arts class, or volunteering, these environments are perfect for meeting like-minded individuals. Shared activities take the pressure off of small talk or forced interactions. Over time, friendships grow as you work, sweat, or learn alongside each other.

Step Three: Show Authenticity

Real friendships go beyond shared interests. They demand authenticity, which requires showing up as you truly are, not who you think others want you to be. Open up about your struggles, vulnerabilities, and fears, even if it feels uncomfortable. Vulnerability isn't a weakness; it's an invitation for others to be real with you. When you let your guard down, you create space for deeper connections. Friendships thrive on mutual trust, and trust is built when both sides feel seen, heard, and valued.

For example, consider how powerful it is to admit to a friend, "I've been feeling lost lately," or "I could really use some advice." Simple statements like these not only make you human but also encourage support from others and strengthen the bond between you.

Step Four: Give Generously

Strong friendships are built on reciprocity and a spirit of giving. Be the kind of man who gives without expecting anything in return. Avoid being stingy. Whether it's advice or material things, give with an abundance mindset. Of course, don't let people take advantage of you. Overall, when you give genuinely—whether it's your time, money, attention, or support—you signal to others that they can trust you. And this creates a ripple effect. The more you give, the more others feel inspired to give back, creating a cycle of mutual support and respect.

Strength in Numbers

The Band of Brothers survived war because they had each other. Unity turned ordinary men into legends. Having said that, the modern day man doesn't have to fight in a war to experience the essential human experience of connection.

Build your band of brothers, invest in your relationships, and you'll find strength, accountability, and purpose that no man can achieve alone. Every man needs a brotherhood. Build yours, and you'll never stand alone.

Chapter 12: Solitude

"Without great solitude, no serious work is possible."
— Pablo Picasso

Why Every Man Must Learn to Walk Alone

It might seem strange to talk about being alone right after discussing brotherhood. If a person does well in the company of others, why would they also need time to be alone? The reality is that these two ideas aren't opposites—they actually support each other.

A man without a brotherhood is isolated. He drifts through life without the sharpening force of other strong men to challenge him. But a man who cannot stand alone is weak. He becomes dependent and needy. A man who is comfortable with solitude builds strength from within. However, many men are terrified of solitude. Afraid of being alone with their thoughts, they try to escape loneliness through social media, distractions, and shallow relationships. True solitude isn't loneliness. Loneliness is feeling disconnected even in a crowd.

Solitude is a choice. It's where a man finds clarity and strength, and where he meets his true self.

In life, there will be many moments when you must walk alone. A man who cannot walk alone will never be truly free. He will be trapped in fear. And when the day comes for him to walk alone he will crumble.

The Buddha: Wisdom Through Solitude

Throughout history, the greatest men have understood the power of solitude. Siddhartha Gautama, known as the Buddha provides an excellent example. Born into wealth and privilege, he was shielded from the harsh realities of life. His father, the king, ensured he lived in luxury, surrounded by comfort, beauty, and endless pleasures. Yet, despite having everything a man could desire, he felt a deep emptiness. He sensed that life had more meaning than pleasure and material success. When he finally went beyond the palace walls,he was confronted with suffering—sickness, aging and death—which shattered his illusions and sparked a desire for something deeper.

Rather than seeking answers from the comforts of his privileged life, Siddhartha did what few men have the courage to do: he walked away from everything. He left behind his royal title, his wealth, and even his family. He withdrew into solitude, choosing instead to wander alone in search of truth. Under the Bodhi tree, in complete solitude, he meditated, stripping away all distractions and facing his thoughts, fears, and desires. It was there, in the depths of self-exploration, that he found enlightenment. He realized that true peace and wisdom come not from chasing pleasure or avoiding pain but from mastering one's mind, detaching from external validation, and understanding the impermanence of all things.

Buddha's journey teaches us that stepping away from the world isn't a sign of weakness. Instead, it can lead to inner strength. Solitude isn't about running away from reality; it's about facing it directly.

What Are You Afraid Of? The Darkness, or What's Inside It?

What are you really afraid of? The silence? The stillness? Or the truth that emerges when there's nothing left to distract you? Most men don't fear solitude itself—they fear what it forces them to confront. Strip away the noise, the scrolling, the constant chatter, and what remains? Your thoughts.

Your regrets. Your insecurities. The things you've buried.

This is why so many men avoid being alone. Silence creeps in. They reach for their phones, turn on the TV, or seek company. Not out of desire, but out of desperation to escape themselves. But the more you run, the stronger the shadows become. And when a man cannot be alone he becomes dependent. He constantly seeks validation, approval, and reassurance from others. His mind weakens. He loses the ability to think deeply, to reflect, to process his emotions, and to truly know himself.

A man must reclaim his ability to stand alone. Not as an act of withdrawal, but as an act of power. Solitude is not isolation; it is ownership of your mind. It is the ability to sit in stillness, to face yourself without fear, and to emerge stronger. Because if you can't be alone with yourself, how can you ever expect to lead your life?

When a man learns to be alone, he unlocks several key benefits:

- **Self-Discovery and Clarity:** When distractions are stripped away, you learn who you really are. You confront your thoughts, desires, and weaknesses without outside influence.

- **Mental Strength and Independence:** A man who is comfortable being alone is not desperate for approval. He stands firm in his beliefs, decisions, and purpose.

- **Mastery and Skill Development:** Solitude allows for deep focus, leading to mastery. Great thinkers, warriors, and artists have all used solitude to achieve great things.

- **Spiritual and Emotional Growth:** Reflection in solitude leads to a deeper understanding of life, mortality, and inner peace.

- **Inner Peace:** True confidence comes from knowing you don't need external validation to feel complete. A man at peace with himself is unstoppable.

- **Creativity and Problem-Solving:** Many of history's greatest ideas and inventions were born in solitude. When the noise of the world is silenced, true insight emerges.

Mastering Solitude Without Losing Connection

Solitude is a powerful tool for self-mastery, but too much of it can lead to isolation. On the other hand, too much social dependence can make a man needy. A strong man understands both solitude and brotherhood. He knows when to stand alone and when to seek support. The key is balance. A man must be comfortable in his company but also able to connect with others when needed.

When the time calls for solitude, embrace it fully. Use it to grow stronger, more focused, and become more self-aware. When the time calls for brotherhood, engage with presence and bring your best self into the relationships you build.

Here are a few ways to make good use of solitude:

- **Schedule Daily Alone Time:** Set aside a portion of each day to be by yourself, free from distractions. Whether it's early morning reflection, an evening walk, or simply sitting in silence, make solitude a habit.

- **Disconnect from Social Media:** Stop seeking validation through likes and digital interactions. Give your mind the space to think deeply rather than being bombarded with external noise.

- **Spending Time in Nature:** Walks in solitude, hikes, or even sitting in quiet surroundings help you break away from the artificial stimulation of modern life and reconnect with yourself.

- **Practice Silent Reflection or Meditation:** Learn to sit with your thoughts, process emotions, and develop inner stillness. This strengthens your mental clarity and emotional resilience.

- **Engage in Deep Work:** Use your alone time for meaningful self-improvement. Read, write, train, or build something with focus and dedication. These activities sharpen your mind, develop discipline, and channel solitude into productive growth.

A Strong Man Does Not Fear Solitude

And nor does he reject the power of brotherhood. He understands that both serve a purpose. One refines his inner strength, and the other sharpens him through the company of men who challenge and elevate him. He walks alone when he must. But he also knows when to stand alongside others.

Mastery of solitude means control, not isolation. The man who can be alone without feeling lonely, who can stand on his own without seeking validation, is truly unshakable. He does not run from stillness or fear his thoughts. He masters it all.

Use solitude as a weapon. Let it sharpen your mind, strengthen your will, and forge you into something greater. Because the man who has mastered solitude has, in truth, mastered himself.

Chapter 13: Health

———— ✦◇◇◉◇◇✦ ————

"It ain't about how hard you hit. It's about how hard you can get hit and keep moving forward."
— Sylvester Stallone

This is Sparta!

In ancient times, few warriors displayed strength like the Spartans. From the moment a Spartan boy turned seven, he was taken from his family and placed into the *agoge*. This was a brutal training system designed to forge him into an unbreakable warrior. Every challenge was designed to push his body beyond its limit, preparing him for a life where only the strong thrived.

The Spartans understood that strength wasn't optional. It was the foundation of survival. Unlike modern men who struggle with motivation and distractions, the Spartans had no choice but to be strong. Every single day of their lives was a test, a constant war against comfort and complacency. Relentlessly, they trained for combat because they knew that their lives and the survival of their people depended on it.

One of the greatest examples of Spartan strength came in 480 BC at the Battle of Thermopylae. King Leonidas and his 300 Spartans stood at the narrow pass of Thermopylae, blocking the path of the mighty Persian army, an army that numbered in the hundreds of thousands. The Spartans knew they were outmatched but in the face of certain death, they fought anyway.

For three days, the Spartans held the line against wave after wave of Persian attacks. The enemy sent their best warriors only to see them cut down by Spartan spears. The battlefield was a slaughterhouse, the ground slick with blood, yet the Spartans did not waver. Seemingly invincible, they moved together as one, shields locked and spears striking with deadly precision.

But they were betrayed. A traitor revealed a hidden path that allowed the Persians to surround the Spartans. Leonidas and his men could have fled or surrendered. But they did neither. Instead, they stood their ground, choosing to fight until the last man. With their backs against the wall, they abandoned their spears and drew their swords, cutting down enemy after enemy in brutal hand-to-hand combat. Even when their blades shattered, they fought with their fists, their teeth. Anything they could use in a fight to the death.

In the end, they fell. But their sacrifice became the spark that ignited Greece to rise up and eventually crush the Persian invasion. The 300 became immortal, their legend echoing through history as the ultimate testament to the power of strength and the will to fight even in the face of certain death.

Train for Life, Not for Looks

The Spartans didn't train for aesthetics. They didn't care about having chiseled abs or python-sized arms. Their bodies were weapons built for endurance and conditioned to survive the harshest realities of battle. Training wasn't about vanity; it was about being stronger than the enemy. A weak body meant a dead warrior. That meant that strength was a necessity and not an option.

Today, many chase fitness for the wrong reasons. Obsessing over Instagram-worthy physiques and vanity metrics. But here's the truth—no one truly cares about your six-pack or big arms. And if they do, so what? You're not building strength to impress others; you're making sure that your body is an asset, not a liability.

Ask yourself: Can you lift your body weight? Can you sprint when necessary? Can you fight if you had to? Can you carry someone to safety in an emergency? If your fitness is built solely on aesthetics, you may look strong but lack the ability to perform when it truly matters. Life is unpredictable, and real strength isn't measured in gym selfies.

Worse than the man chasing vanity is the couch potato who does nothing. A man who lets his body weaken until, one day, he wakes up in a hospital bed. By the time he decides to take his health seriously, the damage is already done. Years of neglect don't just disappear overnight, and unlike a missed gym session, some consequences can't be undone. Don't wait for the wake-up call that comes too late.

To truly reclaim your fitness, shift your focus from aesthetics to ability. Train not for validation, but for capability, resilience, and longevity.

- **Commit to Strength as a Lifestyle:** Physical training isn't something you "try" for a few weeks before quitting. It's a non-negotiable part of life. Whether it's lifting weights, running, martial arts, or bodyweight training, find something challenging and make it part of your life.

- **Fuel Your Body for Performance:** Nutrition doesn't mean restricted eating or obsessing over food; it means giving your body what it needs to thrive. Focus on real, whole foods, lean proteins, healthy fats, and the nutrients that fuel peak performance. Forget crash diets; build sustainable habits.

- **Master Recovery:** The Spartans trained relentlessly, but they also understood the importance of rest and took a strategic approach to recovery. Sleep, mobility work, and stress management aren't weaknesses. They are essential tools for longevity and peak performance.

- **Develop Mental Resilience:** Fitness isn't just about the body. It's about forging a mind that refuses to quit. When workouts get tough, push through. When progress slows, stay the course. Every rep, every sprint, and every mile builds strength beyond the physical.

Sharpen Your Weapon or Let It Rust

Your body is your greatest weapon. Let it weaken, and life may break you. Sharpen it, and you become unstoppable. Again, this isn't about vanity. What matters is whether you have the strength to endure, to fight, and to push forward when it counts. A weak man is at the mercy of life. A strong man bends life to his will.

To become stronger, you don't need a perfect plan—you need action. Choose one area and attack it with the discipline of a warrior:

- **Training Goal:** Strength-train at least three times per week for the next three months.

- **Nutrition Goal:** Cut out processed garbage and fuel your body with real, nutrient-dense food.

- **Recovery Goal:** Prioritize 7 to 8 hours of sleep per night to keep your mind sharp and energy high.

Set the goal, track your progress, and hold yourself accountable. There are no shortcuts or secret hacks. Show up and put in the work. Because at the end of the day, weakness is a choice and so is strength. Choose wisely.

Chapter 14: Intelligence

"Intelligence is the ability to adapt to change."
— Stephen Hawking

Don't Be an Idiot.

Harsh? Maybe. But in a world that's constantly changing, ignorance isn't just a disadvantage—it's a liability. Intelligence goes beyond academics; it's about adaptability, being ahead of the game, and making smart decisions to stay ahead in a competitive society. Without it, you're just getting by, waiting for a break instead of making things happen.

Being healthy is one thing, but as a man, it's also your duty to keep learning, growing, and sharpening your mind. If you think you can get by on charisma, brute force, or past successes, think again. The world doesn't slow down for anyone. Your ability to learn, adapt, and stay relevant is what will determine whether you rise to meet life's challenges or fall behind.

Throughout history, intelligence has been the defining trait of great leaders and innovators. Take Sun Tzu, the ancient Chinese military strategist who wrote *The Art of War*. For him, intelligence wasn't just about knowing the enemy—it was also about understanding yourself, your resources, and the terrain you operated in. He emphasized preparation, adaptability, and the ability to anticipate challenges before they arose. His intelligence manifested in strategies and calculated moves designed to conquer the enemy.

Sun Tzu's lessons on strategy and intelligence have been applied to business, politics, and personal development for centuries. They highlight a timeless truth: intelligence means staying ahead of the world as opposed to reacting to it. Great men have long understood that knowledge isn't static. Learning new ideas and improving their skills enabled them to push the boundaries of possibility.

The Components of Intelligence

Intelligence is far more than just IQ scores or academic credentials. It also encompasses how you approach life's complexities and adapt to its challenges. Lifelong learning is a cornerstone of intelligence. It involves the curiosity and discipline to expand your understanding continually, whether through books, experiences, or meaningful conversations.

Adaptability is another critical component of intelligence. Life will always throw challenges at you. Intelligence is what enables you to pivot and adapt instead of breaking under pressure. It's not about knowing everything. It's about being resourceful and quick to adjust when the unexpected happens. Equally important is strategic thinking. Short-term fixes might get you by, but the ability to see the bigger picture and plan for the long term is a hallmark of true intelligence. Whether you're making career decisions or navigating relationships, strategy beats impulse every time.

Perhaps the most overlooked aspect of intelligence is self-awareness. Knowing your strengths, weaknesses, and blind spots is essential. A man who understands himself can focus on growth where it's needed most. Meanwhile, someone who lacks self-awareness is destined to repeat the same mistakes again and again. You don't have to be perfect; you have to be willing to reflect, learn, and improve

Ignoring the development of your intelligence isn't just a missed opportunity—it's a risk. Falling behind in your career, personal growth, and relationships is only the beginning. A man who neglects to learn and adapt becomes irrelevant in a world that rewards progress. Over time, his irrelevance chips away at his confidence, creating a cycle of stagnation that's hard to escape. But the consequences go deeper. Failing to grow intellectually often leads to a loss of respect, not just from others but also from yourself.

A man who avoids learning and growth becomes trapped by his unwillingness to change. Without intelligence, opportunities pass by, relationships deteriorate, and self-esteem erodes. Meanwhile, the intelligent man attracts opportunities and smart people into his circle.

Building intelligence isn't rocket science, but it does require effort. Here's how to get started:

- **Read, Learn, Apply:** Knowledge is useless if it stays theoretical. Read widely, learn deeply, and apply what you've learned to real-world problems.

- **Stay Adaptable:** Change is inevitable. Embrace it, and find ways to thrive in the face of uncertainty.

- **Develop Skills:** Whether it's learning a new language, mastering a craft, or improving at your job, continuous skill-building keeps you competitive.

- **Network and Learn from Others:** Surround yourself with people who challenge and inspire you. Their perspectives and experiences can broaden your understanding.

- **Self-Evaluate:** Regularly reflect on your decisions and actions. What worked? What didn't? How can you improve?

Stay Sharp

As a man, you owe it to yourself and those who depend on you to stay sharp. Be the man who can lead with clarity, solve problems with creativity, and create a better future for himself and others. Start small. Read a book, learn a new skill, or seek out conversations that challenge your thinking. Over time, these small activities compound, sharpening your mind and setting you apart.

The world doesn't wait for anyone. So, what kind of man do you want to be? The one who adapts, learns, and thrives—or the one who gets left behind? The choice is yours.

Chapter 15: Wealth

"Get rich or die trying."
— Curtis Jackson (50 Cent)

Being Broke Is No Good

Let's be real, no one respects a man who can't handle his business. Whether you like it or not, your ability to build and sustain wealth reflects your discipline, focus, and leadership. Wealth isn't just about buying fancy cars or posting Instagram-worthy vacations. It's about power. Not over others, but over your life.

When you're broke, you don't get to choose because you're trapped, making decisions out of desperation instead of choice. Forget long-term goals when you're drowning in short-term survival. That's not living; that's barely keeping your head above water!

As a man, it's your job to have your money in order. Not because society says so, but because the people who depend on you deserve it and so do you. Wealth isn't a luxury; it's like an oxygen mask. In an emergency, you're told to put yours on first because you can't help anyone else if you're gasping for air. The same applies to money. If you're constantly stressed about bills, debt, and survival, how can you focus on anything else? How can you possibly build anything meaningful?

More money doesn't just mean more stuff. It means more freedom. It's the ability to walk away from a job that drains your soul. It's about protecting the people you love. It's having the resources to handle life's curveballs without falling apart, whether that's a medical emergency, a job loss, or an unexpected crisis. Financial security doesn't mean greed, but peace of mind. It's about peace of mind. It's waking up every day knowing you're in control. That you're not at the mercy of circumstances. That you've built something solid. Not just for yourself, but for the people who count on you.

Stop making excuses! The economy isn't holding you back. Your boss isn't the reason you're stuck. Luck isn't the deciding factor. The harsh truth? It's on you. But that's the good news because it's within your power to change it. Learn new skills, create new opportunities, and shift your mindset. No one's coming to save you, but you don't need them to because you've got everything you need to make it happen.

Historical Perspective: The Role of Providers

John D. Rockefeller's story is the ultimate example of wealth as responsibility. Born in 1839 to modest beginnings in upstate New York, Rockefeller's early life was shaped by a father who was a traveling con artist and a devoutly religious mother who emphasized hard work, frugality, the value of discipline, thrift, and responsibility. These qualities would later define his approach to wealth.

Rockefeller started working as a bookkeeper at the age of sixteen, earning just fifty cents a day. Even in his teenage years, he meticulously tracked every penny he earned and spent. This attention to detail and relentless focus on financial discipline became the foundation of his success.

In 1863, he entered the oil industry and founded what would later be known as the Standard Oil Company. Standard Oil changed the oil industry with new and efficient ideas. They cut down waste, made good deals with railroads, and built a monopoly that controlled the majority of the U.S. oil supply. Some people criticized their business methods as harsh, but they clearly brought stability and efficiency to a chaotic industry.

Rockefeller's true legacy isn't just his wealth, but how he used it. When he retired, he was the richest man in the world. He saw his fortune as a tool to create meaningful change, not just as a goal. Through the Rockefeller Foundation, he funded medical research that led to the eradication of diseases like yellow fever and hookworm in the U.S. In addition, his charitable work helped shape modern philanthropy, focusing on using wealth strategically and effectively to address social issues.

Rockefeller believed in being responsible with his wealth. He was known for his simple habits and didn't flaunt. For him, being wealthy wasn't just for his benefit; it was also for taking care of others.

Building Wealth

Wealth doesn't come by chance. It's not a lottery ticket, a lucky break, or some secret only a few know. It's the result of deliberate action. A man who takes charge of his finances doesn't wait for opportunities to fall into his lap—he creates them. Wealth is earned, not given, and the price is paid in consistency, sacrifice, and smart decisions over time.

Discipline is the foundation. It's the ability to say no when it matters. Saying no to impulse spending and distractions that pull you away from your financial goals. Skipping the fleeting highs of instant gratification for the long-term rewards of financial freedom. Every dollar you save and every investment you make is a building block to a better future. This isn't glamorous, but it's what separates the man who talks about success from the one who lives it.

A relentless work ethic is the engine. Talent and ideas mean nothing without execution. Wealth grows through consistent and focused effort. Whether you're grinding in a career, building a business, or managing multiple income streams, the formula remains the same: show up, do the work, and don't quit when it gets hard. The difference between those who succeed and those who don't isn't always intelligence or skill. Often, it's the refusal to stop when others would. Hard work compounds, just like money. It builds momentum over time, creating opportunities that didn't exist before.

Calculated risks are another cornerstone of wealth-building. Growth requires stepping outside your comfort zone, whether it's launching a business, investing in new opportunities, or negotiating for what you're worth. The key is balancing ambition with caution. Take risks that are informed, not reckless.

Vision is the compass. Without a clear target, you'll drift, working hard but going nowhere. A man with a vision knows exactly what he's building. Maybe it's financial independence, the ability to retire early, or securing a future where your family never has to worry again. Whatever it is, it gives your effort direction. A man with a vision is able to make sacrifices because he knows that it leads to something greater.

Building wealth is only half the battle; keeping it is the other half. Life will throw punches. There will be unexpected expenses, market downturns, personal setbacks. A man who's serious about his wealth doesn't leave himself exposed. He has an emergency fund, diversified investments, and safeguards in place to weather financial storms. He's not just playing offense (chasing growth); he's also playing defense, ensuring that one bad break doesn't wipe out years of progress.

Wealth is Power

But not over others. It's power over your life. The power to walk away from what doesn't serve you. The power to provide and to live life on your terms.

A man who embraces the responsibility of wealth-building creates his reality. A man who ignores his finances is weak.

Financial instability doesn't just limit your lifestyle; it chips away at your confidence, your relationships, and your ability to lead. When money controls you, it dictates your choices. You stay in jobs you hate because you can't afford to leave. You tolerate situations you'd otherwise reject because you're trapped. Financial freedom doesn't necessarily mean that you're rich, but that you have options.

Wealth-building is a journey, not a destination. It isn't just about money—it's about control, freedom, and the legacy you leave behind. Build it with intention, or be ruled by the consequences of neglect.

Chapter 16: Status

———◆◇◇◉◇◇◆———

"It is not titles that honor men, but men that honor titles."
— Niccolò Machiavelli

Why Status Matters

Status. It's the silent force shaping every room you walk into. You feel it before a word is spoken. It's the subtle shifts in body language, the unspoken respect, the way some voices carry weight while others fade into the background. It's the invisible currency that influences relationships, career opportunities, and how much respect you command from the world around you.

Men are constantly being measured and judged based on their status. And here's the uncomfortable truth—if you're not actively building it, you're losing it. But status isn't just about money, fame, or social rank. It runs deeper than that. It's about respect, influence, and the silent authority you project without saying a word. It's the way you carry yourself, the energy you bring, and the standards you uphold.

Some men like to dismiss status as superficial, something only insecure people care about. But that's just an excuse to avoid the hard work. Status doesn't mean feeding your ego, but owning your role in the world. It's a reflection of the value you offer, the respect you command, and the example you set for others. Status isn't given—it's earned. And maintaining it? Well, that's a full-time job.

This chapter is meant for you to understand that status is a tool that can open doors, shape your identity, and influence the world around you. Whether you're leading a team, building relationships, or carving out your place in life, status matters. The question isn't whether it's important or not. The question is—what are you doing about it?

The Master of Power Dynamics: Niccolò Machiavelli

When it comes to understanding status, few men have analyzed it as sharply and effectively as Niccolò Machiavelli. Born in 1469 in Florence, Italy, Machiavelli wasn't a king, a warrior, or a man born into wealth. He was a political advisor, a diplomat, and, most importantly, a master observer of how status shapes influence and respect. His masterpiece, *The Prince*, is often misunderstood as a guide to manipulation. In reality, it's a brutally honest manual for understanding how others perceive your worth and how easily that perception can shift.

Machiavelli lived during a time of constant political change in Florence, a city-state filled with betrayals, shifting alliances, and power struggles. He witnessed how men gained power quickly but also lost it just as fast if they didn't understand the underlying forces at work, one of which was status. To Machiavelli, status wasn't just about holding a title or being in a position of authority. It was more about how others see you, your influence, and your control over their perceptions.

Consider his observations of leaders like Cesare Borgia, the ruthless son of Pope Alexander VI, whom Machiavelli admired for his cunning ability to command respect and fear simultaneously. Borgia wasn't the most charismatic man, nor was he the most morally upright. But he understood one thing better than most: status is about controlling the narrative. He knew when to be generous to win loyalty and when to be ruthless to maintain order. His rise to power wasn't fueled by luck; it was the result of strategic decisions designed to strengthen his position in the eyes of others.

Machiavelli's key lesson? Status is fragile. It can be built over years and destroyed in a single moment. It's not enough to gain status. As a man, you have to maintain it. This requires constant vigilance, self-awareness, and the ability to adapt to changing circumstances. A man who rests on his achievements, assuming his status will sustain itself, is already on the path to losing it.

Why Status Still Matters Today

Status isn't just a thing of the past; it plays a major role in our modern lives— whether in the boardroom, your social circle, or even on social media. Status determines whose opinions matter, whose voices get heard, and whose actions carry weight. Ignoring it doesn't make it go away. In fact, neglecting to manage your status puts you at the mercy of others' perceptions. But while status can open doors, it can also become a trap if you chase it for the wrong reasons.

Chasing status purely for external validation leads to emptiness. Men who base their worth solely on how others perceive them become slaves to those perceptions. They constantly seek approval, lose touch with their true selves, and build fragile identities that crumble under pressure. Many men fall into the trap of believing in surface-level symbols of success like expensive cars, designer clothes, and flashy lifestyles. But status without substance is hollow. It's like building a house on sand; it might look impressive from the outside, but eventually, it collapses under the weight of its emptiness.

Then there's the danger of addiction to approval. If your sense of worth depends entirely on external validation, you'll always be chasing the next hit of approval. Doing this leads to anxiety, burnout, and a lack of genuine confidence because your identity is tied to the fleeting opinions of others. True status doesn't come from applause or attention—it comes from within. It's rooted in self-respect, competence, and living in alignment with your values. External recognition is just the byproduct.

Building Status: The Masculine Approach

A man builds status not by faking confidence and flashing wealth. He does so by becoming the type of man. The masculine approach to status is rooted in self-mastery, discipline, and purpose. It's about creating a foundation so strong that status becomes a reflection of your character—not a fragile mask you constantly need to maintain.

Here's how to build status:

- Master Your Craft:

  Choose something to focus on. It can be your job, a business, a skill, or a personal goal. Work hard to become an expert at it. When you master a skill, you gain confidence and this makes others see you as an authority. People respect competent men.

- Lead, Don't Follow

  Leadership isn't about job titles; it's about influence. Leadership isn't limited to managing teams or running companies. It's involves taking initiative in your life. A man who makes decisions with conviction and stands firm in his values sets an example others naturally want to follow. People respect men who know where they're going.

- Control the Frame

  Your "frame" is the mental space you hold in social dynamics. High-status men control their frame. They don't get rattled by external noise or pulled into petty conflicts. They set the tone. Controlling your frame means staying grounded, emotionally composed, and unshaken by opinions that don't matter. People respect men in control.

- Invest in Your Image

While status runs deeper than appearances, how you present yourself still matters. Dress with intention. Maintain good grooming. Move with purpose. This isn't vanity, it's self-respect. How you show up visually communicates who you are before you say a word. A man who looks sharp, stands tall, and carries himself with confidence sends a clear message: I take myself seriously, and you should too.

Status as a Reflection of Who You Are

At its core, status isn't about titles, possessions, or public recognition. It's about how you show up in the world. It's the respect you command without asking for it, the influence you wield without forcing it, and the legacy you build without shouting about it. True status isn't something you put on like a suit. It's something you become.

When your status is rooted in competence, character, and self-respect, it becomes bulletproof. It doesn't crumble under pressure because it's not built on shallow foundations like fleeting trends or external validation. It's woven into your identity. It's the quiet, unshakable confidence that speaks before you do. And the presence that lingers long after you've left the room.

But here's the hard truth: status is never static. You're either reinforcing it or letting it go. Every decision you make, every habit you form, every standard you uphold—these are the bricks in the foundation of your status. It's not something you achieve once and keep forever. It's a daily practice, a reflection of the man you choose to be when no one's watching. So, the question isn't about whether status matters or not. It's whether you're the one controlling it or letting the world decide it for you.

Don't chase status. Build it, earn it, and live it. Most importantly, become the kind of man who doesn't need to talk about status because it's already written into how he lives.

Chapter 17: Charisma

"Be yourself; everyone else is already taken."
—Oscar Wilde

Why Charisma Matters for Men

Status is one thing, but if people are leaving you on-read, forgetting your name for the fifth time, or only half-listening when you speak, you've got a charisma problem. That girl who ghosted you? She wasn't feeling it. That promotion you didn't get? Maybe they think you're dull. It's not because you're a bad person. It's because you're invisible. And that invisibility stems from one thing: you lack charisma.

Charisma isn't about being the loudest guy in the room or having some movie-star smile. It's about making people feel something when they're around you. It's the ability to command attention without demanding it and to have people remember you. Not because you were flashy, but because you were genuine, engaging, and memorable.

Charisma isn't reserved for the naturally charming. You don't have to be an extrovert or crack jokes every chance you get. Charisma is a skill, and like any skill, it can be learned. If you've ever thought, "I'm just not that guy," you're wrong. With focus and effort, you can become the man people remember. Who doesn't want to be someone people call back and whose name sticks in their minds? The kind of man who walks into a room and leaves an impression that lingers long after he's gone. It's time to stop blending into the background.

That's a Big Desk for a Little Guy

In the early days of Arnold Schwarzenegger's Hollywood career, his search for a breakthrough lead role led him to an interview with Dino De Laurentiis, one of the most legendary producers in the industry. De Laurentiis was a towering figure in Hollywood—figuratively, if not literally. When Schwarzenegger walked into his office, he couldn't help but notice the producer's massive desk. With a mix of humor and unfiltered boldness, he said, "Why does a little guy need such a big desk?"

The room went silent. De Laurentiis, unimpressed, promptly threw Schwarzenegger out of the office. In what became known as the fastest meeting in

Hollywood history, Arnold's boldness had backfired spectacularly. His agent declared it a disaster. But Arnold didn't let rejection define him. Instead, he used moments like this to refine his approach, turning his natural charisma into an asset rather than a liability. While that meeting didn't go as planned, it became a stepping stone on his journey. Along the way, he refined how to connect with people and win them over with his larger-than-life personality.

He went from being mocked for his thick Austrian accent to becoming one of the most recognizable figures in the world. Whether it was inspiring millions through his bodybuilding achievements, charming audiences on the big screen, or winning over California voters as the "Governator," Arnold's charisma was a key ingredient in his success.

The Components of Charisma

Charisma is often mistaken for confidence, but it's much more than that. It's not about dominating or trying too hard to impress. It's about creating an undeniable presence that lingers long after you've left. At its core, charisma is the energy you bring into every interaction. It's the subtle mix of confidence, authenticity, and emotional connection that makes people lean in, listen, and remember you.

Arnold didn't become a global icon because he had the perfect line every time. He became one because he understood how to refine the charismatic elements that made people gravitate toward him. And here's the good news: you don't need an accent, a bodybuilding title, or a blockbuster film to do the same. Charisma isn't magic or something you're born with. In fact, it can be broken down into five core components.

1. Confidence

Charisma begins with confidence in yourself. You don't need to be the loudest voice in the room or act like you know everything; true confidence comes from carrying yourself with self-assurance, even when you're uncertain. People are naturally drawn to those who seem confident. Arnold's ability to walk into any room and hold his ground is a perfect example of how confidence can be magnetic.

2. Authenticity

People can spot a fake smile a mile away. Authenticity means owning who you are and being genuine in your interactions. Arnold's larger-than-life personality worked because it was real. He embraced his accent, his humor, and his unique perspectives. When you're unapologetically yourself, people gravitate toward you because they know they're dealing with someone real.

3. Listen

Charisma is more than talking; it involves listening too. Listening allows you to connect with people on a deeper level by showing that you care about their thoughts and feelings. When you genuinely listen, people feel valued and understood. Overall, this builds trust and makes you memorable.

4. Body Language

Your presence is communicated as much through your body as your words. Open gestures, strong posture, and genuine eye contact convey charisma. Arnold mastered body language, whether on stage during bodybuilding competitions or in political debates. Through his physical presence, he always projected charisma.

5. Storytelling

A charismatic man knows how to tell a story. Whether it's recounting a personal failure or painting a vision of the future, storytelling creates an emotional connection. Arnold's ability to weave his immigrant story into his successes made him relatable, inspiring millions to believe that hard work and determination could lead to greatness.

How to Build Magnetic Charisma

Understanding charisma is one thing, but living it is another. Real transformation happens when you apply it. It goes beyond having a few charming moments. It's becoming the kind of man who naturally draws people in, whether you're in a boardroom, on a date, or just making small talk at a coffee shop.

So, how do you cultivate this magnetic presence? Well, it begins with deliberate practice, and takes consistent effort, the right techniques, and a willingness to step outside your comfort zone. Your goal is to uncover the most confident, authentic version of who you already are.

Let's break down how you can sharpen this skill and turn your presence into something people can't ignore.

1. Improve Communication

Charismatic people speak with clarity and conviction. Avoid filler words like "um" and "uh," and instead pause when you want to let your words land. Practice slowing down your speech to project confidence and control. But don't forget communication isn't just about talking. Active listening is equally powerful. Lean in slightly when someone speaks, nod to show you're engaged, and ask thoughtful follow-up questions. People are drawn to those who genuinely listen because it makes them feel seen and heard.

2. Master Your Body Language

Body language speaks louder than words. Stand tall with your shoulders back and chest open. This stance doesn't just signal confidence to others but it reinforces it within yourself. Make deliberate, controlled movements. Avoid fidgeting because it shows nervousness. Eye contact is crucial—not the aggressive stare-down, but steady, natural eye contact that conveys both confidence and warmth. And never underestimate the power of a genuine smile, it disarms tension, builds rapport, and makes you more approachable.

3. Develop Confidence Through Action

Confidence isn't a feeling that appears out of thin air; it's the result of action. The more you do, the more capable you feel. Regularly step outside of your comfort zone. Speak up in meetings even when you're nervous. Strike up conversations with strangers, or take on leadership roles that stretch your limits. Each small victory builds your self-belief. Confidence isn't the absence of fear—it's the willingness to act despite it.

4. Practice Storytelling

Facts inform, but stories inspire. Learn to tell your story in a way that resonates. You don't need to be a master orator—just be authentic. Share personal experiences, especially moments of struggle and growth. People connect with vulnerability because it's real. Use vivid language, create tension, and end with a lesson or takeaway that inspires others. A compelling story can turn a simple conversation into a memorable connection.

5. Cultivate Authenticity

Charisma without authenticity is manipulation. Magnetic people are unapologetically themselves. They don't put on an act to impress others; they lean into who they are. Identify your values and live by them. Don't be afraid to show your flaws. After all, they make you more human and relatable. Moreover, it encourages others to be authentic, which leads to genuine connections.

Charisma in Everyday Life

Charisma isn't just for actors, politicians, or influencers. It's for every man who wants to leave a mark. It shows up in the small moments. The conversation with a stranger, the way you hold yourself in a meeting, or how you connect with your partner after a long day. It's the invisible thread that pulls people in, makes them want to listen, and leaves them feeling like they've just met someone who matters.

In relationships, it's not all about smooth talk but making the other person feel genuinely seen and heard. In business, it's about making people believe in you. In life, it's the quiet confidence that speaks louder than words.

But here's the truth most people won't tell you: You don't have to be perfect to have charisma. You simply have to be present. Fully engaged. No distractions, no pretenses. The ripple effect of that presence is undeniable. A man who shows up—authentic, confident, grounded—doesn't need to demand respect. He earns it without trying.

So, start small. Speak with purpose. Listen like it matters—because it does. Carry yourself like your presence alone is enough—because it is. Charisma isn't something you're born with. It's something you build, brick by brick, through self-awareness, intention, and showing up as the realest version of yourself.

Chapter 18: Leadership

—— ◆◇◇◉◇◇◆ ——

"Lead me, follow me, or get out of my way."
— George S. Patton

The Fall of a King Without a Crown

Julius Caesar walked through the streets of Rome, a city he had taken over with vision, charm, and strong leadership. The people there loved him. As he walked by, they cheered and praised him as their leader who brought order to Rome's chaos.

Despite all his victories and power, he was walking toward his death. At the entrance to the Senate, a man stepped forward and handed him a note. A warning. It was a list of conspirators plotting to kill him. But he didn't read it. He stepped into a room filled with men he had once called allies. Men he had spared. Men he believed still respected him. Then, the first blade struck.

It was Casca, one of his closest allies. Caesar turned, shocked, reaching out in defense, but then another blade came, and then another. He had no guards and no protection. He never thought he would

151

need them. Backward, he staggered, blood pouring from his wounds. He locked eyes with Brutus, the man he had trusted above all others, the man whose life he had once spared.

"Et tu, Brute?" he whispered.

And then, he fell.

Julius Caesar, the greatest general Rome had ever seen, the man who had reshaped history, died in a pool of his own blood. Not on the battlefield, but in a Senate chamber filled with men who had once followed him. In the end, it wasn't an army or a rival that brought him down. It was his failure to see the threats within his own ranks, his refusal to listen, and his belief that he was untouchable.

His story is a warning: Leadership isn't only about taking control—it's also about keeping control. Many men have made the same mistakes as Caesar. They believed their past victories would protect them, that power alone made them great, and that they wouldn't need to adapt. But true leadership requires more.

A man who leads does not just command—he inspires. He does not just seize power—he protects and nurtures it. He does not just seek followers—he builds them into something stronger. The difference between great leaders and those who fall is simple: mastery of self, mastery of vision, and mastery of responsibility.

And this is where your journey as a leader begins.

The Role of Leadership in Masculinity

Every man, at some point in his life, will be called to lead. It may be in his career, his family, his friendships, or even within his community. Great leaders don't wait for others to take charge; they step forward, make decisions, and set the tone for those around them. But leadership isn't granted automatically. It's earned through actions, through consistency, and through the way a man carries himself. A true leader doesn't demand respect—he inspires it and leads by example. The world doesn't lack men in leadership positions. What it lacks are men who embody true leadership.

Today, many men struggle with leadership. Not because they lack ambition, but because they are unsure of what leadership truly means. Society has blurred the lines, making men hesitant to take charge, afraid of being too dominant or too passive. They are told to lead, yet are criticized for being too assertive. They are told to be decisive, yet are warned about being too controlling.

Such confusion has left many men uncertain of when to take charge and when to step back. The truth is, real leadership has nothing to do with ego, dominance, or seeking control over others. It's about being the foundation, the steady hand in times of chaos, and the man people trust when things get difficult.

The Foundations of Leadership

A strong leader embodies key qualities that make him someone others respect, trust, and follow. Luck or birthright has nothing to do with it. Leadership it is forged through action, sharpened by adversity, and strengthened over time. These are the pillars of leadership that define a man's ability to lead. Master them, and you'll be a leader in every aspect of your life:

1. Vision: The Ability to See Beyond the Present

A leader isn't consumed by the present moment. He looks ahead. He has a clear sense of purpose and direction. Whether leading a business, a family, or himself, a man must have a vision that guides his decisions.

- What kind of life are you building?

- Where do you want to be in five, ten, or twenty years?

- How do your daily actions align with that vision?

A leader without vision is a man drifting through life. A leader with vision is a man who sets goals, plans his path, and takes action with intent.

2. Responsibility: The Willingness to Own the Outcome

A leader never blames others. He takes full responsibility for his successes and failures. Weak men make excuses. Strong men own their results.

- If your business fails, own it and learn from it.

- If your relationship struggles, examine your role in it.

- If you are out of shape, take responsibility for your health.

A man who blames others gives away his power. A man who takes responsibility is in control of his destiny.

3. Decisiveness: The Courage to Make Tough Choices

Indecision is the enemy of leadership. A weak man hesitates and is afraid to make mistakes. A strong man gathers information, trusts his instincts, and makes a firm decision. This doesn't mean acting recklessly. It means weighing the risks, considering the consequences, and moving forward with confidence.

- In business, indecisiveness costs time and money.

- In relationships, indecisiveness creates doubt and instability.

- In personal growth, indecisiveness leads to wasted potential.

A true leader understands that making a wrong decision is often better than making no decision at all. He learns, adapts, and moves forward.

4. Integrity: Leadership Through Character

A leader's word is his bond. If people cannot trust your word, they cannot trust your leadership. Integrity means:

- Following through on what you say.

- Being honest, even when it's difficult.
- Holding yourself to a higher standard than those around you.

Integrity builds loyalty. A man who is trustworthy, who does what he says he will do, and who stands by his principles will always be respected.

5. Strength: The Ability to Stay Steady in Chaos

A leader must be a rock. When others panic, he remains calm. When times are tough, he becomes even tougher.

Strength is not just physical—it's mental and emotional resilience. It's the ability to handle pressure without breaking, to endure hardships without losing focus.

- A leader does not complain.
- A leader does not fold under stress.
- A leader stands firm, even when others around him crumble.

People follow men who are unshakable. If you can maintain composure under pressure, others will look to you for leadership.

6. Adaptability: The Ability to Lead Through Change

No plan survives contact with reality. A true leader understands this and remains adaptable.

- Businesses collapse. Leaders rebuild.
- Relationships struggle. Leaders navigate through it.
- Life throws curveballs. Leaders adjust and keep moving.

Stubbornness is not strength. The strongest leaders evolve, adjust and keep their vision alive despite facing challenges.

Lead Your Life

Becoming a leader doesn't require a title, a position, or permission. Leadership starts in the way you carry yourself, the way you make decisions, and the way you show up every day. Before you can expect others to follow you, you must first lead yourself.

A man who lacks discipline in his life cannot lead others. If your health is failing because of neglect, if your work ethic is weak, or if your word means nothing, how can you expect anyone to trust you as a leader? True leadership begins with self-mastery.

Take control of your habits, sharpen your discipline, and develop the strength to do what needs to be done—even when no one is watching.

Weak men hesitate, fearing mistakes, waiting for the perfect moment. But a true leader understands that the perfect moment never comes. He makes decisions with the best information available, trusts his instincts, and commits to action. Indecision leads to stagnation, and stagnation leads to failure. Start small—set a goal, make a choice, and follow through without hesitation. If you fail, own it, learn from it, and move forward. Every decision you make strengthens your ability to lead.

A true leader doesn't only focus on himself—he lifts others up. Whether in business, friendships, or family, the strongest men help those around them grow. A great leader doesn't hoard knowledge or power; he shares it, mentors others, and holds his people accountable. He builds, he teaches, and he strengthens the people he leads. Leadership isn't about being alone at the top—it's about creating something greater than yourself.

Leadership isn't easy. It requires hardship, responsibility, and an acceptance of pressure. Weak men run from challenges, avoiding discomfort. Strong men seek it out, knowing that the struggle is what builds them. The more adversity you face, the more capable you become. Leadership is forged in fire. The more you embrace it, the stronger you will become.

The world is filled with men who wait. Waiting for permission, for opportunity, for someone else to take charge. But history is written by men who lead.

Decide today: Will you lead, or will you follow?

Hey!

If you want to go beyond reading and actually apply what's in this book, I've created a full online course called Masculinity Reforged.

You can join it here:

tommy-s-school34.teachable.com/p/masculinity

Chapter 19: Gluttony

———— ✦◇◇◉◇◇✦ ————

"To govern oneself is the greatest power of all."
— Lao Tzu

The Fall of Hitler

History is filled with men whose ambitions led them to greatness. It is also filled with those whose greed led to their destruction. Adolf Hitler stands as one of history's most infamous examples of gluttony in its most destructive form. Not in food or drink, but in his insatiable thirst for power, conquest, and domination. Had he focused on strengthening Germany alone, his grip on power might have lasted longer. Millions were loyal to him, and had the ability to reshape his nation. But it wasn't enough. He wasn't satisfied with restoring Germany; he wanted all of Europe. His insatiable hunger for more led him to overreach and make critical errors that would ultimately seal his demise.

Hitler's fatal mistake came during the invasion of the Soviet Union in 1941. He had already conquered much of Europe, defeating France and pushing Britain to the brink. But instead of consolidating his power and securing his empire, he launched Operation Barbarossa, an all-out attack on the Soviet Union. It was a decision fueled by arrogance and an unchecked desire for more territory, more dominance, and more control. The German army, initially successful, soon found itself bogged down in the brutal Russian winter—ill-equipped, underprepared, and facing an enemy that refused to break. What could have been a manageable empire turned into an overstretched disaster.

Hitler had ignored the lessons of history. Napoleon had met the same fate in Russia over a century earlier. But gluttony blinds men to reality. Thus, he pressed forward, obsessed with total conquest, and in doing so, he doomed himself. By 1945, the once-dominant Third Reich was in ruins. Hitler's empire crumbled not because of external enemies alone, but because he refused to recognize one fundamental truth—more is not always better.

The Modern Man's Battle with Excess

Gluttony is often related to overeating, but its true nature runs far deeper. It's the insatiable hunger for more. More food, more pleasure, more distractions, and more power. It's a weakness that can manifest in many forms, from endless consumption to reckless ambition. Just as Hitler's inability to be satisfied with what he already had led to his ruin, modern men often fall into the same trap. Not with warfare, but with overindulgence.

In today's world, excess is everywhere. Food, entertainment, instant gratification—all within arm's reach. We no longer have to struggle for survival. We don't need to hunt, build, or endure. The result? A generation of men growing weaker. Not because of war or famine, but because they can't say no to themselves.

Gluttony doesn't just lead to weight gain or laziness. It leads to a slow erosion of control. When a man consistently gives in to indulgence, he trains himself to be weak. Every unnecessary bite, every indulgent craving satisfied without thought, is another step toward losing mastery over himself.

Consider the consequences:

- **Physical Weakness:** A body burdened by excess becomes slow, lethargic, and inefficient. Strength and vitality are replaced with sluggishness and health issues.

- **Mental Fog:** Overconsumption, whether of food, media, or comfort, dulls the mind. The ability to think sharply, plan ahead, and stay focused is eroded by the need for constant stimulation.

- **Diminished Willpower:** Every time you indulge without restraint, you train yourself to submit to impulse. A man who cannot resist an extra plate of food will struggle to resist other temptations, whether in business, relationships, or personal development.

- **Loss of Self-Respect:** If you cannot command yourself, how can you expect to lead others? A man who lacks control over his appetites will also find control slipping away in other areas of his life.

Gluttony is the silent enemy of masculinity, undermining its core virtues—discipline, self-restraint, and purpose. A man who allows excess to take root in his life becomes ruled by his impulses rather than his vision. Instead of commanding his desires, he is controlled by them, losing the strength and clarity that define true masculinity.

Breaking Free from the Excess Trap

A man should never be at the mercy of his desires. It's a bottomless pit. The more you indulge, the more you crave. A man who eats for comfort never reaches a point where he's truly "full." A man who chases casual sex to fill an emotional void never finds lasting fulfillment. The momentary high fades, leaving behind an even greater hunger. This is why desire, when left unchecked, becomes a cycle of diminishing returns. Every time you give in, the satisfaction lasts a little less, and the emptiness grows a little more.

Men often indulge in excess to escape discomfort—boredom, stress, loneliness, or frustration. Rather than confronting their challenges, they numb themselves with food, alcohol, entertainment, or other indulgences. But avoidance isn't a strategy. You don't conquer your struggles by drowning in pleasure; you conquer them by facing them with discipline and action. Hunger, boredom, stress—these aren't enemies to avoid; they're signals to listen to. Instead of reacting impulsively, sit with them and let them pass.

Train yourself to resist the automatic pull of indulgence. When you fast, you're not just improving your health—you're proving to yourself that your appetite doesn't own you. When you cut out mindless consumption—whether it's binge-eating, binge-watching, or scrolling for hours—you reclaim the energy wasted on meaningless indulgence.

Regaining control isn't about living in denial; it's about consuming with intention. When a man indulges without purpose, he becomes a slave to his desires. But when he dictates when, how, and why he indulges, he regains power over himself. Moderation is the key. Food should fuel your body, not become an escape from boredom. Sex should deepen connection, not become a meaningless pursuit of validation. Entertainment should add value, not serve as a distraction from an unfulfilled life.

The world will always tempt you with more. Be the man who rises above it. Choose restraint over indulgence, purpose over excess, and strength over weakness. Your appetite should serve you, not rule you. True power is knowing when enough is enough.

Master your appetite, and you master your life.

Chapter 20: Gratitude

———— ✦◇◇◉◇◇✦ ————

"Acknowledging the good that you already have in your life is the foundation for all abundance."
— Eckhart Tolle

Gratitude: The Strength in Appreciation

When the constant hunger for more is no longer in control, something else takes its place. A deeper recognition of what's already there. Gratitude. It's a word that often feels overused and oversimplified, like something you say before a meal or when you receive a gift. But gratitude is far more than just politeness. It's a mindset, a way of seeing the world that can transform your life. In a world where people want more, it helps us remember what we already have. Know that it's not about wanting less; it's about knowing that what we have is enough.

For men, gratitude can be a powerful tool. It's not just about saying "thank you" when someone does you a favor. It's about acknowledging the relationships, experiences, and opportunities that shape you. Doing so builds emotional strength, keeps you grounded, and reminds you of what really matters. Ultimately, it makes you a better partner, friend, and leader.

Gratitude isn't a new concept. It's been a cornerstone of human philosophy and spirituality for centuries. From soldiers in battle to leaders in crisis, gratitude has long been a source of strength and clarity. The Stoics, for example, believed that gratitude was essential for happiness. Marcus Aurelius regularly reflected on what he was grateful for, even amid the weight of ruling an empire. Buddhist teachings also emphasize gratitude, encouraging mindfulness of the present moment and appreciation for life. Native American traditions weave gratitude into daily life, offering thanks to the earth, the sky, and the animals for their contributions.

We Have It Too Easy

Today, we are standing on the shoulders of those who came before us. Mentors who guided us, loved ones who supported us, and ancestors who fought for opportunities we now take for granted. Life today is easier than ever. Just a hundred years ago, people had to grow their food, gather water, and travel for days to get things that we can now have in minutes with a simple click or swipe. While this convenience shows how far we've come, it has also turned us into a society that takes things for granted.

When things come easily, we value them less. A meal delivered to your door in twenty minutes doesn't carry the same weight as one prepared by your own hands. Swiping through endless streaming options doesn't feel as satisfying as finding a hidden gem in a bookstore or video shop. Fundamentally, when it comes to easy, we disconnect from the effort and meaning behind what we consume.

Being grateful doesn't require you to live in a cave and own nothing. You should still strive for more, but at the same time, you should appreciate what you already have. A grateful man understands that and appreciates his journey. He accepts the highs and the lows, finding gratitude in it all.

The Benefits of Gratitude

Gratitude isn't just a nice feeling. Studies have shown that individuals who consistently practice gratitude report fewer symptoms of depression and anxiety. They face life's challenges with a grateful mindset, which fosters resilience. When you regularly acknowledge the positives in your life, your brain rewires itself to notice more of them, which, in turn, creates a cycle of optimism.

Gratitude benefits extend beyond the mind and into the body. Grateful people often sleep better because their minds aren't racing with worry or dissatisfaction before bed. Additionally, gratitude is linked to a stronger immune system and lower levels of inflammation and stress. Grateful individuals are also more likely to engage in healthy behaviors and respect their well-being.

Gratitude doesn't merely improve your internal world—it strengthens your external connections. Expressing gratitude for others builds deeper, more meaningful relationships. It signals to others that you recognize and value them. Naturally, this strengthens your relationships. People who regularly express gratitude are perceived as being warmer, which attracts stronger social networks. In leadership roles, gratitude enhances team morale and promotes a positive, collaborative environment.

Practical Ways to Cultivate Gratitude

Gratitude isn't something you either have or don't have. It's a skill you can build with practice. Just like physical strength, mental habits grow stronger the more you work on them. Here are some practical ways to integrate gratitude into your daily life:

1. Gratitude Journaling

One of the simplest and most effective practices is gratitude journaling. Set aside five minutes each day to write down three things you're grateful for. They don't have to be profound. For example, small things like a good conversation, a sunny morning, or a warm cup of coffee count just as much as major life events. The key is consistency. Over time, this habit rewires your brain to naturally focus on the positives in your life, shifting your perspective from scarcity to abundance.

2. The "Three Blessings" Exercise

At the end of each day, think about three moments that made you grateful. They could be as simple as a smile from a stranger, completing a task you'd been putting off, or unexpectedly hearing your favorite song. By actively seeking out these moments, you train your mind to recognize the good, even during challenging times.

3. Expressing Gratitude in Relationships

Gratitude isn't just an internal practice; it thrives when shared with others. A simple, heartfelt "thank you" can go a long way, but take it a step further. Be specific; tell someone how much you appreciate them. Specificity makes gratitude feel more genuine, and regularly expressing it builds a positive atmosphere in any relationship.

4. Mindful Gratitude Moments

Throughout your day, pause for brief moments of mindfulness. Whether you're sipping your morning coffee, feeling the warmth of the sun on your face, or hearing laughter nearby—stop and take a breath. Acknowledge the simple beauty in these everyday experiences. This practice keeps you grounded, reminding you that gratitude isn't only reserved for big milestones—it's woven into the fabric of daily life.

The Challenges of Practicing Gratitude

Practicing gratitude won't always be easy. When you're facing setbacks, it can seem distant, even hollow. But that's precisely when it holds the most power. That doesn't mean that you ignore your struggles or sugar-coat your reality. Gratitude doesn't require you to pretend everything is fine when it's not. It requires you to look deeper, to find something that reminds you you're still standing, still fighting, and still here. When everything feels like it's falling apart, gratitude is the anchor that keeps you grounded. It's the quiet realization that even in the darkest moments, there's a flicker of light, or a part of you that refuses to break.

Some days, your gratitude might be for something simple, a hot cup of coffee, a moment of silence, the breath in your lungs. On other days, it might be for lessons learned the hard way or for the people who stood by you. Over time, these acknowledgments build momentum. Fundamentally, they shift your focus from what's missing to what's present, from scarcity to abundance, and from despair to hope.

The more you practice gratitude, the more you'll realize that it isn't about settling for less. It's about realizing how much you already have, even when life gets challenging. And that's where its real power lies: not in making life perfect, but in reminding you that even in imperfection, there's beauty. Even in struggle, there's strength. And even in loss, there's something left to hold on to.

But gratitude alone isn't enough. Recognizing what matters is just the first step. The next step? Refining your life—eliminating what holds you back, sharpening what moves you forward, and ensuring that everything you allow into your world serves a purpose.

A great life isn't just built on appreciation; it's built on intentionality. And that begins with ruthless refinement.

Chapter 21: Refine

"Everything in your life—your thoughts, habits, relationships, and environment—either serves you or it does not. If it does not serve you, eliminate it."

—Darcy Carter

The Ruthless King

A great king doesn't tolerate weakness in his court. He doesn't allow traitors, thieves, or fools to sit at his table. He doesn't let his castle fall into ruin by ignoring what must be repaired. A man's life is his kingdom, and yet most men allow corruption, weakness, and dead weight to thrive inside their walls. They hesitate, making excuses for the things that hold them back, refusing to eliminate what no longer serves them.

A king who fails to rule with clarity and strength will watch his empire fall. If a law doesn't serve the kingdom, it's rewritten. If a man betrays the mission, he is exiled. If a system is broken, it's torn down and rebuilt stronger. This isn't cruelty—it's survival.

Your life demands the same iron hand. Every thought, habit, relationship, and environment in your world is either strengthening your rule or leading you toward collapse. If something doesn't serve you, it's your enemy. This is the cost of building a kingdom worth ruling.

You Selfish Bastard!

You think you can just cut people out of your life because they aren't useful to you anymore? You think you're a king, deciding who stays and who goes? What about loyalty? What about compassion?"

This is the argument the weak will throw at you. The ones who have never built anything worth protecting. The ones who live in mediocrity and who let their lives crumble because they lack the spine to make the hard choices. They tell you that eliminating what doesn't serve you is cold, ruthless, and selfish. But here's the truth:

It is selfish. And it should be.

Because if you don't guard your time, energy, and focus, the world will consume them for you. If you don't enforce the standards of your kingdom, it will fall into ruin. A king who refuses to exile traitors, dismiss the unworthy, or rewrite the laws of his land doesn't remain a king for long. His people lose faith. His enemies move in. His empire collapses. And what was once strong rots from the inside out.

Most men live like weak rulers—allowing their past, their fears, and their attachments to dictate their decisions. They let bad people linger in their lives too long, slowly zapping their vitality. They let habits stay that no longer serve their mission. They hold onto outdated versions of themselves or mediocrity because of comfort.

And then they wonder why they feel powerless.

The greatest act of loyalty you can have is to your mission. Your responsibility isn't to every person who has ever crossed your path. It's not to every version of yourself that once existed. Your responsibility is to the empire you are building. The weak call it cruel. The powerful call it necessary.

Live a Life That Serves You

A man should build his life with intent, and it must serve him. Every part—his habits, his environment, his relationships—it all must serve him. Anything that doesn't serve him must be eliminated. Your home, your routines, the media you consume—do they serve you? Do they contribute to your growth, your strength, your ambition? Or do they make you comfortable, stagnant, and weak?

A king doesn't fill his palace with distractions. A warrior doesn't carry extra weight into battle. Every item in your life, every person in your circle, and every minute of your time should have a purpose. If it doesn'tt, it's working against you. If you wake up in a cluttered space, surrounded by things that belong to the man you used to be, you're anchoring yourself to the past. If you spend your time consuming meaningless entertainment, engaging in pointless conversations, or indulging in habits that steal your energy, you're actively weakening yourself.

Look at your routines. Do they serve you? Do they build your discipline? Do they move you toward your goals? If not, they must be restructured or removed.

Look at your circle. Do they serve you? Do they challenge you, sharpen you, push you to be better? Or do they waste your time, drain your energy, and encourage your complacency?

A man should surround himself only with that which makes him stronger. Anything else is a distraction, and distractions are dangerous. Your time, your energy, and your focus are not infinite.

They must be spent with intention. Every decision should be made with one question in mind:

Does this serve me? If the answer is no, it does not belong in your life.

Cutting Out the Dead Weight

Refinement means subtracting, not adding. A sculptor doesn't create by stacking more clay onto a block; he removes everything that does not belong. The same applies to your life. If something isn't actively making you stronger, sharper, better, or more focused, it's dead weight. And dead weight must be cut away.

- **Relationships:** People either elevate you or drain you. There is no obligation to keep people in your life simply because they have always been there. If someone disrespects you, constantly brings negativity, or holds you back, they are a liability. Cut them loose.

- **Habits:** Every habit is a vote for the man you are becoming. If a habit doesn't contribute to your success, your health, or your mindset, it doesn't belong in your life. If it slows you down, if it makes you comfortable in your weakness, it must be eliminated.

- **Thoughts:** Your mind is either your greatest ally or your greatest enemy. Limiting beliefs, self-doubt, and excuses are the silent assassins of progress. Weak men accept their negative thoughts as truth. Strong men confront them, deconstruct them, and replace them. If a thought doesn't serve you, it's not yours to keep.

Stop Making Excuses

Refinement will not be easy. It will require confrontation, not avoidance. It will demand that you stop making excuses for the things that hold you back and that you take full responsibility for every aspect of your life. Most men know what they need to do. They hesitate not because they are confused, but because they are afraid. Afraid of confrontation, afraid of loss, afraid of change. Holding onto what no longer serves you is weakness. It is not noble, and it is not kind. It is self-betrayal. Walking away from a job, a relationship, or a way of life that does not serve you is not loss—it is freedom.

A man who clings to the past is a man who will never own his future. Strength is knowing when to let go. A man must serve himself first before he can serve anyone else. Strength is not built by pouring yourself into things that weaken you. True power comes from cutting out distractions, eliminating waste, and focusing entirely on what makes you better.

The greatest men in history operated with clarity. They did not waste time. They did not entertain mediocrity. And they did not let themselves be burdened by things that did not serve their mission. You must do the same.

Refinement is a brutal process. But it is necessary and it never ends. If something does not serve you, it is gone. No hesitation. No guilt. No exceptions.

Chapter 22: Reforged

———————◆◇◇◉◇◇◆———————

"He who has a why to live can bear almost any how."
— Friedrich Nietzsche

The Philosopher Who Challenged the World

Friedrich Nietzsche was born in 1844 in Röcken, Germany, into a strict religious household where discipline, structure, and faith shaped his early years. But as he grew, he did what few dared to do. He questioned everything. Not just the beliefs he was taught, but the very foundations of morality, religion, and human purpose. While most sought comfort in conformity, Nietzsche pursued the harshest truths, even if it meant standing alone against the world.

His writings weren't meant to soothe. They were meant to provoke, challenge, and unsettle. He saw blind obedience to societal norms as intellectual laziness. He didn't just ask, "What do you believe?" He asked, "Why do you believe it?" His critiques of religion, morality, and culture forced people to confront uncomfortable truths about themselves and the systems they lived under.

Nietzsche saw then that most people drift through life, shackled by expectations they never chose, afraid to question them because doing so would mean stepping into the unknown. His work wasn't for those who wanted easy answers. It was for those who had the courage to create their own reality in a world that constantly pressures them to fit in.

Today, Nietzsche's ideas are still relevant because they touch on something timeless: the battle to live with authenticity. To go beyond inherited beliefs, to question your limits, and to confront the uncomfortable truths you'd rather ignore. Real fulfillment doesn't come from playing it safe, avoiding failure, or seeking approval. It comes from facing the internal battle and committing to becoming the strongest version of yourself.

The Ubermensch: Rising Beyond Limitations

One of Nietzsche's most well-known ideas is the concept of the *Übermensch*, or the "Overman." He described the *Übermensch* as an individual who transcends traditional morals and limitations, creating his own values and forging his own path. To Nietzsche, this was the highest achievement of human potential. Becoming a man who dictates his destiny rather than following the expectations imposed by society.

The *Übermensch* doesn't seek approval; he creates his own reality. In a world that rewards conformity, Nietzsche reminds us that true fulfillment comes from the courage to embrace our uniqueness. Such transformation demands discomfort. It requires letting go of inherited beliefs, taking full ownership of one's actions, and committing to a life of purpose.

Modern men can apply this principle by shifting their focus from external validation to internal growth. But before that, you need to ask yourself some hard questions: Who are you really? Are your beliefs, desires, and goals truly your own, or are they the product of societal brainwashing? Were you raised to be a certain kind of man because that's what others expected, or have you chosen your path with full awareness? Overcoming this conditioning is essential to becoming who you want to be and how you want to live. Without it, you are simply a product of the system, not the architect of your life.

Everything else in this book will help you with that, but it starts with breaking free from the expectations that have been placed on you. But self-overcoming is only part of the story. True evolution is not just about surpassing external barriers. It's about confronting the hidden, often uncomfortable parts of ourselves. And this brings us to one of Nietzsche's most profound ideas: the courage to face, integrate, and harness all aspects of who we are.

Beyond Good and Evil

Nietzsche's work challenges traditional notions of morality, encouraging individuals to move beyond rigid categories of "good" and "evil" and embrace the complexity of their nature. He believed that true strength comes from integrating all aspects of oneself, both the light and the dark. Darkness can be a driving force, and when directed with purpose, it can become a source of immense power. Instead of fearing the shadows within, explore them. Understand them and harness their power.

Every man carries darkness within him—rage, ambition, jealousy, fear. Society teaches men to suppress these feelings, to label them as "bad" or "unmanly." But when you bury what you fear, it doesn't disappear. It festers. Instead, face that darkness head-on. Learn from it and harness it. Anger can become courage when directed with purpose. Fear can sharpen your instincts.

Embracing the darker parts of yourself doesn't mean losing control or becoming consumed by them. It's about integration. The same man who channels his anger into action must also be able to sit with his vulnerability without shame. Strength isn't the absence of vulnerability, and sensitivity isn't a weakness.

True masculinity is about balance. It's not about fitting into a box labeled "strong" or "sensitive"— it's about being both when the moment calls for it. That involves accepting your contradictions, your light, and your dark and realizing that these paradoxes are not weaknesses—they are the foundation of your strength.

Practical Strategies for Self-Overcoming

Self-overcoming isn't an abstract ideal; it's a daily practice at becoming a better man. To grow, you should try new things and not be afraid to feel uncomfortable.

Here's how to start applying the principles of self-overcoming in your everyday life:

- **Cultivate a Growth Mindset:** Make it a habit to choose the difficult path over the easy one, whether it's pushing your limits in the gym, taking on new responsibilities at work, or having difficult conversations. Growth happens outside your comfort zone.

- **Develop a Discipline Routine:** Nietzsche believed that discipline is essential for self-mastery. Set clear goals, establish daily habits that support them, and hold yourself accountable.

- **Question Your Beliefs:** Challenge inherited values and societal expectations. Take time to reflect on what truly matters to you and build your life around those principles. Don't just blindly follow what others expect of you.

- **Master Your Emotions:** Learn to observe your thoughts and feelings without being controlled by them. Practices such as mindfulness and journaling can help develop emotional intelligence and self-awareness.

- **Eliminate Excuses:** The journey to self-overcoming requires complete ownership of your actions. Excuses and procrastination are barriers to progress. Replace them with action and accountability.

- **Surround Yourself with Growth-Oriented Individuals:** The people you spend time with will influence your mindset and behaviors. Seek out those who challenge you, inspire you, and support your pursuit of excellence.

- **Do This Quick Exercise:** Identify one area of your life where you've been settling for comfort. Write down three actions you can take this week to push yourself beyond that limit.

Create Your Own Reality

The greatest battle a man will ever fight isn't against the world—it's against himself.

Every day, you're faced with two choices: to remain bound by the limits imposed on you, or to break them. To accept the beliefs, habits, and expectations that were handed to you, or to strip them away and forge your own. Most men never make that choice consciously. They go through life reacting instead of creating, following instead of leading, surviving instead of truly living.

Nietzsche's philosophy of self-overcoming wasn't about small improvements within the framework of an existing life. It was about tearing that framework down and building something entirely new. It was about refusing to be shaped by external forces and instead shaping yourself from within. He saw strength not as something you inherit, but as something you create through struggle, discipline, and relentless action.

Most men will never do this. They will wait, hoping for the world to change around them, for the right moment, the right opportunity, the right permission. But no one is coming to save you. No one will hand you a life of meaning. The only way forward is to seize control and create it yourself.

This is your life. Your mind. Your future. You can either let it be shaped by forces outside your control, or you can become the architect of your reality.

And once you have done that—once you have reforged yourself into something stronger—the next question is: What will you do with that strength? How will you leave your mark on the world?

Chapter 23: Legacy

———— ◆◇◇◉◇◇◆ ————

"It is in your hands to make
a better world for all who live in it."
— Nelson Mandela

Nelson Mandela's Legacy of Forgiveness

Nelson Mandela was born on July 18, 1918, in the small village of Mvezo on the Eastern Cape of South Africa. Growing up, he saw the unfair treatment of Black South Africans under apartheid, a harsh system that enforced racial segregation and stripped millions of their dignity and basic rights. Motivated to fight for change, Mandela dove into education and politics, ultimately joining the African National Congress (ANC) in 1944. This marked the beginning of a lifelong commitment to fighting for liberty and justice. But when peaceful protests were met with violence, he made the difficult decision to embrace armed resistance. In 1964, he was sentenced to life imprisonment for his actions, and it seemed his fight for justice had come to an end.

Yet, in the quiet isolation of his prison cell on Robben Island, Mandela's legacy was taking shape. Rather than being bitter, he used his twenty-seven years of imprisonment to reflect, grow, and refine his vision for a united South Africa. True change, he realized, wouldn't come through revenge but through reconciliation. His transformation during those years wasn't only personal but deeply strategic. Locked away, he prepared himself to lead a nation out of hatred and into hope.

When Mandela was released in 1990, he faced a country divided and close to civil war. Yet he did not seek revenge against those who had jailed him. Instead, he promoted forgiveness and invited his former enemies to join in discussions to unite South Africa. As the first Black president, he used his role to encourage healing, end apartheid, and support a new era of democracy.

Mandela's legacy was built on forgiveness, compassion, and the belief that humanity is strongest when united. He showed us that a true legacy is not only about awards or fame. It is also about the lives you impact and the positive changes you create.

The Modern Problem: A Life Without Legacy

Today, many men are caught up in the demands of their jobs, financial pressures, and daily tasks. Society values short-term achievements such as social media likes, work promotions, and material possessions. As a result, we're conditioned to seek quick wins, whether that's through career promotions, financial gains, or online recognition. Ultimately, it has distracted men from their purpose and long-term goals. Metaphorically speaking, they are digging a tunnel without looking where they are going.

Pressure to constantly achieve in the present leaves little space for thinking about building a legacy. Moreover, building a legacy requires patience, consistency, and a willingness to invest in long-term efforts that may not provide immediate results. Indeed, this can feel overwhelming or even impossible. Thus, many men drift through life without a firm understanding of what truly matters to them. Without a personal philosophy or guiding principles, they make reactive decisions. As a result, life can then feel like a series of disconnected events rather than a meaningful journey.

Many men hold themselves back from building a legacy because they believe it has to be something world-changing. This misconception leads to inaction. They think that if greatness isn't achieved immediately, it's not worth pursuing. But legacy isn't about size; it's about significance.

The real problem is that most men never take the time to define what they stand for. Instead of shaping their lives with purpose, they drift, reacting to circumstances rather than creating their path. They chase success without ever stopping to ask what success truly means to them.

In the end, a man isn't defined by wealth, titles, or accomplishments but by the impact he leaves. A man builds a legacy through intentional action, not chance. He doesn't wait for the perfect opportunity or hopes history will remember him. He lives in a way that matters now.

Fame, fortune, and recognition mean nothing if they don't leave something lasting. A legacy is about impact— knowing that when you are gone, the world, your family, or even just one person is better because of what you built, what you stood for, and how you lived.

But clarity must come before commitment. You cannot build a legacy if you don't know what you're building. The first step is defining it for yourself.

Practical Exercise: Write Your Legacy Statement

A legacy statement is a clear declaration of what you want your life to stand for. It defines your values, aligns your actions with your long-term vision, and ensures that the impact you leave is intentional. Your legacy isn't something that happens by chance. It's something you build, starting now.

Step 1: Reflect on Your Values

- What do you want to be remembered for?
- Which qualities or principles are most important to you?
- How do you want to impact the people around you?

Step 2: Visualize Your Legacy

- What stories do you want people to tell about you when you're no longer there?
- Who do you hope to have influenced or inspired?

- What changes do you want to have contributed to?

Step 3: Write Your Statement

Condense your thoughts into a single sentence or short paragraph. For example:

- "I want to be remembered as a man who led with integrity, uplifted others, and left the world a little better than I found it."
- "My legacy will be one of courage and kindness, defined by the lives I've touched and the love I've shared."

Live with Purpose, Leave a Legacy

Legacy isn't reserved for the extraordinary. It's built in the quiet moments, in the decisions you make when no one is watching, in the way you carry yourself day after day. It is not a grand declaration, nor is it written in headlines. It's forged through commitment to something greater than yourself.

Nelson Mandela's life teaches us that even the most profound legacies aren't built through personal ambition alone but through our impact on others. He suffered, endured, and emerged from his trials not with bitterness but with a mission. His legacy wasn't an accident. It was a choice, repeated daily, to stand for something larger than himself.

The reality is that every man leaves a legacy whether he realizes it or not. The question is: are you leaving one worth remembering?

There is no guarantee of how long you will have, but there is a guarantee that time will pass. What you build, how you lead, and how you choose to show up in this world will outlast you.

Your legacy is being written right now. Make sure it's one worth reading.

Chapter 24: Honor

"Death Before Dishonor."
— Ancient warrior philosophy

The Weight of Honor

Honor has built civilizations, forged leaders, and separated winners from losers. It's the invisible force that defines a man's place in the world. Without it, a man drifts, betrays his principles, and compromises himself and others. With it, he stands firm—unshaken by external pressures—and leaves behind a name that commands respect.

Throughout history, men have lived and died by their code of honor. The samurai of Japan followed Bushido, the "Way of the Warrior," a strict code that placed honor above life itself. For a samurai, dishonor was a fate worse than death. The same code of honor echoed across cultures: the Spartan warriors, the knights of medieval Europe, and the Roman centurions all upheld it as the ultimate measure of a man.

Honor is not obsolete. The battlefields have changed—from war to business, relationships, and personal choices—but their weight remains the same. In a world where values shift, loyalty is rare, and deception is rewarded, living with honor is a deliberate choice. It separates the strong from the weak, leaders from followers, and those who control their destiny from those controlled by others.

To be a man of honor today is to set a firm standard for yourself. It means keeping your word, even when it's inconvenient. It means standing by your principles, even when it costs you. It means living in such a way that when your name is spoken, it carries weight.

Samurai and the Price of Honor

For the samurai, Bushido, the "Way of the Warrior," dictated every aspect of their lives. It was a strict moral code that placed honor above all else. A warrior's word was sacred, and his actions were a reflection of his character. To break an oath, to fail in battle, or to act in disgrace was to bring shame not only upon himself but upon his family, his ancestors, and his lord. The weight of this dishonor was unbearable. The only way to cleanse oneself of such disgrace was through *seppuku*—ritual suicide.

Seppuku wasn't an act of despair but one of redemption. A samurai who had failed in his duty could reclaim his honor by taking his life with precision and dignity. It was a brutal yet disciplined ritual, often performed in the presence of witnesses, ensuring that the warrior's final act would be one of control, resolve, and courage. The pain was secondary to the principle: he would die with honor rather than live in shame.

Samurai would rather charge into certain death than surrender because survival at the cost of integrity wasn't survival at all. Even in times of peace, the ethos remained. Betrayal, cowardice, or disloyalty were seen as worse than death itself. A man's name was everything, and once it was stained, no riches, no power, and no second chances could erase the dishonor.

Honor in the Modern World

Today, few men live with honor. Society has softened, and dishonor no longer carries the same consequences it once did. Social media rewards deception, clout-chasing, and performative virtue, while true integrity is overlooked or even mocked. In a time when people can rewrite their past with a few clicks, the weight of a man's word has been cheapened.

Dishonor isn't always dramatic or obvious. It manifests in small, everyday compromises:

- Lying to avoid consequences rather than facing the truth.

- Betraying friends or family for personal gain or convenience.

- Being fake—projecting an image instead of standing on real principles.

- Seeking approval over truth, shaping opinions based on what is popular rather than what is right.

- Running from accountability, making excuses instead of taking responsibility.

While no one is immune to these pressures, each act of dishonor chips away at a man's self-respect. It leads to regret, broken relationships, and a reputation that cannot be repaired. Every choice either strengthens or erodes honor—there is no middle ground. A man can break his word, betray his principles, and deceive others without immediate repercussions. However, while the external consequences may be less severe, the internal damage remains. A man who discards his integrity loses something far greater than status or reputation: he loses himself.

Why Reclaiming Honor is Essential

Honor is not a relic of the past—it is the foundation of strong men and strong societies. Without it, trust dissolves, leadership fails, and the bonds that hold people together weaken. A man of honor stands apart in any era, not because he seeks to be different, but because he refuses to abandon what matters.

To live with honor today is to reject the path of least resistance. It means keeping your word, even when no one is watching. It means being truthful, even when dishonesty would be easier. It means standing firm, even when the world urges you to bend.

Honor is not something you claim. It is something you build through consistent action, discipline, and commitment to principles. Here are the essential steps to living with honor.

1. Define Your Code

A man without a clear code is easily swayed. What are your non-negotiable values? What principles will you stand by, no matter the cost? Honor begins with defining the standards you refuse to break.

2. Keep Your Word

Your word is your bond. Never make a promise lightly, and never break one. If you say you will do something, do it. A man's reputation is built on his reliability—once you prove yourself untrustworthy, your word loses value.

3. Always Tell the Truth

Lies weaken the man who speaks them. Speak the truth, even when doing so would be difficult, unpopular, or costly. A man of honor values truth over convenience and earns respect by standing by what is real.

4. Stand by Your People

Loyalty is a rare trait in today's world. Whether in friendships, business, or romantic relationships, don't betray those who trust you. True loyalty isn't blind obedience but a commitment to the values and people who have earned it.

5. Face Fear with Courage

Honor requires courage. The world is full of pressure to conform, deceive, and take the easy way out. A man of honor faces adversity, danger, and hard decisions without retreating. He does not seek comfort—he seeks what is right.

6. Protect Your Reputation

Your reputation is your legacy. Once stained, it's nearly impossible to restore. Act in a way that, if your actions were made public, you wouldn't be ashamed. Carry yourself with dignity, and refuse to engage in behavior that compromises your name.

7. Command Respect Through Actions

Respect is not demanded; it is earned. A man of honor treats others with respect because he respects himself first. He does not belittle, manipulate, or tolerate disrespect toward himself. His presence commands respect because he carries himself with dignity.

8. Stay Disciplined

Without discipline, honor is impossible. A man of honor keeps his commitments, follows through on his promises, and does not allow laziness or excuses to dictate his actions. His word is not flexible—it is final.

9. Accept Responsibility

Own your actions. When you make a mistake, admit it. When you fail, learn from it. Never shift blame or make excuses. The strongest men acknowledge their failures and use them as fuel to improve.

10. Embrace Sacrifice

Honor often comes at a cost. Sometimes, you must give up personal comfort, ease, or temporary gain for a greater cause. Whether protecting your family, standing by your values, or making difficult choices for the sake of others, a man of honor understands that his duty is greater than his desires.

Becoming a Man of Honor

Honor is the foundation of strong men. It separates leaders from followers, the respected from the forgotten. A man of honor doesn't bend to convenience, nor does he compromise his principles for temporary gain. He holds himself to a standard that doesn't shift with the times.

Living with honor means choosing the harder path. It means keeping your word when it would be easier to break it, speaking the truth when it would be safer to lie, and standing firm when others fold. It is not about perfection—it is about consistency, about refusing to compromise what matters.

A man without honor is already dead. His words are meaningless, his relationships are shallow, and his life is dictated by fear and convenience. But a man who chooses honor builds a name that carries weight, a reputation that commands respect, and a legacy that lasts beyond his lifetime.

The choice is clear: live with honor or let it fade.

Conclusion

— ◇◇◉◇◇ —

"Life is a storm. One minute, you will bathe under the sun, and the next, you will be shattered upon the rocks. That's when you shout, "Do your worst, for I will do mine!" and you will be remembered forever."

— Alexandre Dumas, author of
The Count of Monte Cristo

Masculinity Is Not Toxic

Masculinity isn't outdated. It doesn't need to be dismantled, softened, or redefined to fit into the fragile frameworks of temporary trends. It's a force that evolves and rises to meet the demands of every era. It's the quiet strength that stands firm when everything else crumbles. It's the discipline that shapes a meaningful life. It's the unrelenting purpose that drives men to greatness.

For centuries, men have risen to meet the challenges of their time. Not because they were told how to be men, but because they represented timeless principles. They built civilizations from nothing, led revolutions, explored uncharted territories, protected their families, and sacrificed for something greater than themselves. They didn't need validation from society to know their worth: their actions spoke for them.

Yet today, many men find themselves lost in a world that sends mixed messages about what it means to be a man. Strength is mistaken for aggression. Ambition is seen as arrogance. Vulnerability is encouraged, yet mocked when displayed. In this environment, it's easy for men to feel disconnected from their true potential, questioning their identity and their place in the world.

The truth is, masculinity doesn't need to be "reclaimed." It's never gone anywhere. It's been buried under layers of doubt, confusion, and cultural noise. But it's still there. It's in the man who wakes up before dawn to chase a vision no one else believes in. It's in the father who sacrifices his comfort to secure a future for his children. It's in the man who stands alone, unwavering, when his values are tested. It's in every struggle, every setback, every moment when quitting was easier, but he didn't.

The Blueprint for a Fulfilled Life

This book wasn't written to hand you easy answers or quick fixes. It was written to challenge you. To strip away the noise, the excuses, the distractions and to remind you of the timeless principles that have shaped strong men.

We've explored masculinity not as a hollow label but as a way of living. It's breaking free from limitations, embracing personal responsibility, and forging your own identity, as opposed to fitting into society's ever-changing molds. Masculinity is not something you're given. It's something you build— day by day, choice by choice. It's tested in moments of adversity, refined through struggle, and proven not by words but by deeds.

At the heart of this transformation are principles that have stood the test of time. Not motivational slogans or trite quotes. They're the very same principles that have guided men who built empires, led revolutions, protected their families, and left legacies that still echo throughout history. They're the difference between merely existing and truly living with intention, power, and purpose.

Becoming the man you're meant to be isn't about chasing perfection; it's about relentless progress. It's about waking up every day with a simple, brutal question: "Am I better than I was yesterday?" The contents of this book weren't designed to inspire temporary motivation. They were crafted to ignite lasting change. Emotional mastery, discipline, resilience, leadership, brotherhood, legacy—these aren't checkboxes on a list. They are lifelong pursuits.

But here's the harsh truth: reading this book changes nothing. Action does. If you take nothing else from these pages, remember this: progress starts with action.

Not tomorrow. Not when life feels easier. Now.

Pick one lesson. Just one. Whether it's cultivating discipline, standing firm in your values, strengthening your relationships, or facing your fears—apply it today. Small actions done consistently create unstoppable momentum. Every disciplined decision sharpens your character. Every setback faced with resilience strengthens your resolve. Every moment of discomfort embraced with courage pulls you one step closer to the man you're meant to be.

This book isn't the conclusion of your journey. It's the beginning. Masculinity isn't a destination. It's a lifelong process of becoming—of falling, rising, learning, evolving. It's the courage to face your reflection, to acknowledge your flaws without making excuses, and to do the hard work required to grow.

No one is coming to save you.
No one owes you anything.
No one will hand you the life you want.
You have to take it.

Your life will be defined by the choices you make when no one is watching, by the standards you hold when it's hardest to hold them, and by the actions you take, not when it's convenient, but when it's necessary.

The world doesn't need more men who play it safe, stay comfortable, or blend into the background. The world needs men who are grounded, capable, and courageous. Men who lead with strength and integrity. Men who inspire not with their words, but with their actions. Men who refuse to settle for mediocrity when excellence is within reach.

So, who will you be?

The choice is yours.
The time is now.
Your life is your message.
Make it count.

Forge ahead with purpose, live with intention, and master yourself.

The journey starts with you—now.

Ready to Go Beyond the Page?

This book will challenge you to think deeply—but real transformation happens when you take action.

To help you with that, I've created a course called **Masculinity Reforged**.

It is a guided experience with structured exercises, journaling prompts, and real-world challenges to help you apply the lessons inside this book and more.

MASCULINITY REFORGED THE COURSE

⬇️ ⬇️ ⬇️

tommy-s-school34.teachable.com/p/masculinity

References

Chapter 1: Evolution

Lee, B. (1975). *Bruce Lee: The Tao of Gung Fu*. Tuttle Publishing.

Aristotle. (350 B.C.). *Nicomachean Ethics*. Clarendon Press.

Beauvoir, S. (1949). *The Second Sex*. Vintage.

Confucius. (479 B.C.). *The Analects*. Dover Publications.

Donovan, J. (2012). *The Way of Men*. Dissonant Hum.

Tomassi, R. (2013). *The Rational Male*. CreateSpace Independent Publishing Platform.

Xenophon. (375 B.C.). *The Spartan Constitution*. Harvard University Press.

Chapter 2: Purpose

Ford, H. (1922). *My Life and Work*. Doubleday, Page & Company.

Buddha. (500 B.C.). *The Dhammapada*. Oxford University Press.

Collins, J. (2001). *Good to Great: Why Some Companies Make the Leap... and Others Don't.* Harper Business.

Holiday, R. (2016). *Ego Is the Enemy.* Portfolio.

Khan, G. (1206). *The Secret History of the Mongols.* China Intercontinental Press.

Peterson, J. (2018). *12 Rules for Life: An Antidote to Chaos.* Random House.

Pressfield, S. (2002). *The War of Art: Break Through the Blocks and Win Your Inner Creative Battles.* Black Irish Entertainment.

Sinek, S. (2009). *Start with Why: How Great Leaders Inspire Everyone to Take Action.* Penguin Books.

Tolle, E. (1997). *The Power of Now: A Guide to Spiritual Enlightenment.* New World Library.

Chapter 3: Discipline

Willink, J. (2017). *Discipline Equals Freedom: Field Manual.* St. Martin's Press.

Willink, J. (2015). *Extreme Ownership: How U.S. Navy SEALs Lead and Win.* St. Martin's Press.

Clear, J. (2018). *Atomic Habits: An Easy & Proven Way to Build Good Habits & Break Bad Ones.* Avery.

Covey, S. R. (1989). *The 7 Habits of Highly Effective People: Powerful Lessons in Personal Change.* Free Press.

Holiday, R. (2019). *Stillness is the Key*. Portfolio.

Maxwell, J. C. (2011). *The 5 Levels of Leadership: Proven Steps to Maximize Your Potential*. Center Street.

Duhigg, C. (2012). *The Power of Habit: Why We Do What We Doin Life and Business*. Random House.

Chapter 4: Resilience

Churchill, W. (1941). *Speech to the House of Commons, June 4, 1940*. Retrieved from [source].

Churchill, W. (1940). *We Shall Fight on the Beaches*. Speech. Retrieved from https://winstonchurchill.org/resources/speeches/

Gilbert, M. (1991). *Winston Churchill: A Life*. Holt Paperbacks.

Roberts, A. (2018). *Churchill: Walking with Destiny*. Viking.

Snyder, T. (2010). *Bloodlands: Europe Between Hitler and Stalin*. Basic Books.

Stoltz, P. G. (1997). *Adversity Quotient: Turning Obstacles Into Opportunities*. John Wiley & Sons.

Chapter 5: Emotions

Frankl, V. (1946). *Man's Search for Meaning*. Beacon Press.

Aurelius, M. (2002). *Meditations (G. Long, Trans.)*. Penguin Books. (Original work published ca. 170 CE)

Robertson, D. (2019). *How to Think Like a Roman Emperor: The Stoic Philosophy of Marcus Aurelius*. St. Martin's Press.

Irvine, W. B. (2009). *A Guide to the Good Life: The Ancient Art of Stoic Joy*. Oxford University Press.

Sellars, J. (2003). *Stoicism*. University of California Press.

Seddon, K. (2005). *Stoic Serenity: A Practical Course on Finding Inner Peace*. CreateSpace Independent Publishing Platform.

Fowers, B. J. (2010). *The Evolution of Virtue: Human and Stoic Excellence in Moral Development*. American Psychological Association.

Chapter 6: Courage

Schwarzenegger, A. (2012). *Total Recall: My Unbelievably True Life Story*. Simon & Schuster.

Ali, M. (1975). *The Greatest: My Own Story*. Random House.

Brené, B. (2015). *Daring Greatly: How the Courage to Be Vulnerable Transforms the Way We Live, Love, Parent, and Lead*. Avery.

Holiday, R. (2019). *Courage Is Calling: Fortune Favors the Brave*. Portfolio.

Maxwell, J. C. (1998). *Failing Forward: Turning Mistakes into Stepping Stones for Success*. Thomas Nelson.

Sinek, S. (2014). *Leaders Eat Last: Why Some Teams Pull Together and Others Don't*. Portfolio.

Chapter 7: Humility

Gandhi, M. (1927). *The Story of My Experiments with Truth*. Navajivan Trust.

Carnegie, D. (1936). *How to Win Friends and Influence People*. Simon & Schuster.

Collins, J. (2001). *Good to Great: Why Some Companies Make the Leap... and Others Don't*. Harper Business.

Dalai Lama & Cutler, H. C. (1998). *The Art of Happiness: A Handbook for Living*. Riverhead Books.

Holiday, R. (2020). *Ego Is the Enemy*. Portfolio.

Maxwell, J. C. (2007). *The 21 Irrefutable Laws of Leadership: Follow Them and People Will Follow You*. HarperCollins Leadership.

Tolle, E. (1997). *The Power of Now: A Guide to Spiritual Enlightenment*. New World Library.

Chapter 8: Kindness

Bartlett, S. (2022). *Happy Sexy Millionaire: Unexpected Truths About Fulfillment, Love, and Success.* HarperCollins.

Carnegie, A. (1889). *The Gospel of Wealth.* The North American Review.

Collins, J. (2001). *Good to Great: Why Some Companies Make the Leap... and Others Don't.* Harper Business.

Grant, A. (2013). *Give and Take: Why Helping Others Drives Our Success.* Viking.

Holiday, R. (2019). *Stillness Is the Key.* Portfolio.

Johnson, D. (n.d.). "Kindness isn't soft. It's the hardest thing in the world." [Public statement/interview].

Maxwell, J. C. (2007). *The 21 Irrefutable Laws of Leadership: Follow Them and People Will Follow You.* HarperCollins Leadership.

Trivers, R. (1971). *The Evolution of Reciprocal Altruism.* The Quarterly Review of Biology, 46(1), 35-57.

Chapter 9: Honesty

Confucius. (5th Century BCE). *The Analects.* (A. Waley, Trans.). Vintage Classics.

Harris, S. (2014). *Waking Up: A Guide to Spirituality Without Religion*. Simon & Schuster.

Harris, S. (2019). *Meditation for Fidgety Skeptics: A 10% Happier How-to Book*. Spiegel & Grau.

Kabat-Zinn, J. (1994). *Wherever You Go, There You Are: Mindfulness Meditation in Everyday Life*. Hyperion.

Thich Nhat Hanh. (1991). *Peace is Every Step: The Path of Mindfulness in Everyday Life*. Bantam.

Chiesa, A., & Serretti, A. (2010). *A Systematic Review of Neurobiological and Clinical Features of Mindfulness Meditations*. Psychological Medicine, 40(8), 1239-1252. https://doi.org/10.1017/S0033291709991747

Goleman, D., & Davidson, R. J. (2017). *Altered Traits: Science Reveals How Meditation Changes Your Mind, Brain, and Body*. Avery.

American Psychological Association. (2020). *Mindfulness Meditation: A Research-based Perspective*. Retrieved from https://www.apa.org.

Baer, R. A. (2003). *Mindfulness Training as a Clinical Intervention: A Conceptual and Empirical Review*. Clinical Psychology: Science and Practice, 10(2), 125-143.

World Health Organization. (2022). *Mental Well-Being: Mindfulness as a Tool for Mental Health.* Retrieved from https://www.who.int.

Chapter 10: Love

Augustine, S. (1991). *Confessions.* Oxford University Press.

Baumeister, R. F., & Vohs, K. D. (2004). *Handbook of Self-Regulation: Research, Theory, and Applications.* Guilford Press.

Deida, D. (1997). *The Way of the Superior Man: A Spiritual Guide to Mastering the Challenges of Women, Work, and Sexual Desire.* Sounds True.

Freud, S. (1905). *Three Essays on the Theory of Sexuality.* Basic Books.

Gray, J. (1992). *Men Are from Mars, Women Are from Venus: The Classic Guide to Understanding the Opposite Sex.* HarperCollins.

Greene, R. (1998). *The 48 Laws of Power.* Viking Press.

Hill, N. (1937). *Think and Grow Rich.* The Ralston Society.

Napoleon, J. (1852). *Napoleon's Letters to Josephine.* H.S. Nichols.

Perel, E. (2006). *Mating in Captivity: Unlocking Erotic Intelligence*. HarperCollins.

Schopenhauer, A. (1851). *Essays and Aphorisms*. Penguin Classics.

Sinek, S. (2009). *Start With Why: How Great Leaders Inspire Everyone to Take Action*. Portfolio.

Wright, R. (1994). *The Moral Animal: Why We Are the Way We Are*. Pantheon Books.

Chapter 11: Brotherhood

Shakur, T. (1996). *All Eyez on Me*. Death Row/Interscope Records.

Ambrose, S. E. (1992). *Band of Brothers: E Company, 506th Regiment, 101st Airborne from Normandy to Hitler's Eagle's Nest*. Simon & Schuster.

Aristotle. (4th century BC). *Nicomachean Ethics*. Oxford University Press.

Dunbar, R. (1996). *Grooming, Gossip, and the Evolution of Language*. Harvard University Press.

Haidt, J. (2006). *The Happiness Hypothesis: Finding Modern Truth in Ancient Wisdom*. Basic Books.

Putnam, R. D. (2000). *Bowling Alone: The Collapse and Revival of American Community*. Simon & Schuster.

Seneca. (65 AD). *Letters from a Stoic*. Penguin Classics.

Shakespeare, W. (1599). *Henry V*. Penguin Classics.

Chapter 12: Solitude

Picasso, P. (1935). *Statements on Art*. Yale University Press.

Aurelius, M. (180 AD). *Meditations*. Penguin Classics.

Buddha. (5th century BC). *The Dhammapada*. Oxford University Press.

Carlson, R. (1997). *Don't Sweat the Small Stuff... and It's All Small Stuff*. Hyperion.

Frankl, V. E. (1946). *Man's Search for Meaning*. Beacon Press.

Jung, C. G. (1953). *Collected Works of C.G. Jung, Volume 6: Psychological Types*. Princeton University Press.

Kierkegaard, S. (1849). *The Sickness Unto Death*. Penguin Classics.

Merton, T. (1955). *No Man Is an Island*. Harcourt Brace.

Thoreau, H. D. (1854). *Walden or, Life in the Woods*. Ticknor and Fields.

Chapter 13: Health

Stallone, S. (2006). *Rocky Balboa: The Underdog Story.* MGM.

Glassman, G. (2002). *What Is Fitness?.* CrossFit Journal.

Greene, R. (1998). *The 48 Laws of Power.* Viking Press.

Kaczynski, T. (1995). *Industrial Society and Its Future.* The New York Times.

Kraemer, W. J., & Zatsiorsky, V. M. (2006). *Science and Practice of Strength Training.* Human Kinetics.

Leonidas, K. (480 BC). *Accounts of the Battle of Thermopylae.* Greek Historical Records.

Rippetoe, M. (2005). *Starting Strength: Basic Barbell Training.* Aasgaard Company.

Spartan Society Records. (5th century BC). *Agoge Training System.* Greek Archives.

Tversky, A., & Kahneman, D. (1974). *Judgment Under Uncertainty: Heuristics and Biases.* Science.

Chapter 14: Intelligence

Hawking, S. (1988). *A Brief History of Time.* Bantam Books.

Carroll, S. B. (2005). *Endless Forms Most Beautiful: The New Science of Evo Devo and the Making of the Animal Kingdom.* W. W. Norton & Company.

Carson, B. (1996). *Think Big: Unleashing Your Potential for Excellence.* Zondervan.

Dweck, C. S. (2006). *Mindset: The New Psychology of Success.* Random House.

Greene, R. (2012). *Mastery.* Viking Press.

Harari, Y. N. (2014). *Sapiens: A Brief History of Humankind.* Harper.

Kahneman, D. (2011). *Thinking, Fast and Slow.* Farrar, Straus and Giroux.

Plato. (4th century BC). *The Republic.* Penguin Classics.

Senge, P. M. (1990). *The Fifth Discipline: The Art and Practice of the Learning Organization.* Doubleday.

Taleb, N. N. (2012). *Antifragile: Things That Gain from Disorder.* Random House.

Chapter 15: Wealth

Jackson, C. (50 Cent). (2003). *Get Rich or Die Tryin'.* Shady/Aftermath/Interscope.

Babylonian, A. (1926). *The Richest Man in Babylon.* Penguin Books.

Buffett, W. (2008). *The Essays of Warren Buffett: Lessons for Corporate America.* Cunningham Group.

Carnegie, A. (1889). *The Gospel of Wealth.* Carnegie Foundation.

Dalio, R. (2017). *Principles: Life and Work.* Simon & Schuster.

Hill, N. (1937). *Think and Grow Rich.* The Ralston Society.

Kiyosaki, R. (1997). *Rich Dad Poor Dad: What the Rich Teach Their Kids About Money That the Poor and Middle Class Do Not!.* Warner Books.

Munger, C. T. (2005). *Poor Charlie's Almanack: The Wit and Wisdom of Charles T. Munger.* Donning Company.

Rockefeller, J. D. (1909). *Random Reminiscences of Men and Events.* Doubleday.

Taleb, N. N. (2012). *Antifragile: Things That Gain from Disorder.* Random House.

Thiel, P. (2014). *Zero to One: Notes on Startups, or How to Build the Future.* Crown Business.

Chapter 16: Status

Machiavelli, N. (1532). *The Prince.* Oxford University Press.

Cialdini, R. B. (2001). *Influence: The Psychology of Persuasion*. HarperBusiness.

Greene, R. (1998). *The 48 Laws of Power*. Viking Press.

Greene, R. (2012). *Mastery*. Viking Press.

Marcus Aurelius. (180 AD). *Meditations*. Penguin Classics.

Nietzsche, F. (1887). *On the Genealogy of Morality*. *Cambridge University Press*.

Plato. (4th century BC). The Republic. Oxford University Press.

Seneca. (65 AD). *Letters from a Stoic*. Penguin Classics.

Sun Tzu. (5th century BC). *The Art of War*. Oxford University Press.

Tolle, E. (1997). *The Power of Now: A Guide to Spiritual Enlightenment*. New World Library.

Chapter 17: Charisma

Wilde, O. (1882). *The Soul of Man Under Socialism*. Penguin Classics.

Cialdini, R. B. (2001). *Influence: The Psychology of Persuasion*. HarperBusiness.

Fox Cabane, O. (2012). *The Charisma Myth: How Anyone Can Master the Art and Science of Personal Magnetism*. Penguin.

James, W. (1890). *The Principles of Psychology*. Henry Holt & Co.

Koch, R. (1997). *The 80/20 Principle: The Secret to Achieving More with Less*. Doubleday.

Schwarzenegger, A. (2012). *Total Recall: My Unbelievably True Life Story*. Simon & Schuster.

Chapter 18: Leadership

Patton, G. S. (1947). *War as I Knew It*. Houghton Mifflin.

Cialdini, R. B. (2001). *Influence: The Psychology of Persuasion*. HarperBusiness.

Greene, R. (1998). *The 48 Laws of Power*. Viking Press.

Greene, R. (2012). *Mastery*. Viking Press.

Machiavelli, N. (1532). *The Prince*. Oxford University Press.

Maxwell, J. C. (1998). *The 21 Irrefutable Laws of Leadership*. HarperCollins.

Sinek, S. (2014). *Leaders Eat Last*. Portfolio.

Tzu, L. (4th century BC). *Tao Te Ching*. Penguin Classics.

Willink, J., & Babin, L. (2015). *Extreme Ownership: How U.S. Navy SEALs Lead and Win*. St. Martin's Press.

Chapter 19: Gluttony

Tzu, L. (4th Century BCE). *Tao Te Ching*. (S. Mitchell, Trans.). HarperCollins.

Goebbels, J. (1948). *The Goebbels Diaries*. Doubleday & Company.

Hitler, A. (1925). *Mein Kampf*. Houghton Mifflin.

Kershaw, I. (2000). *Hitler: 1936–1945: Nemesis*. W. W. Norton & Company.

Lao Tzu. (4th century BC). *Tao Te Ching*. Penguin Classics.

Marcus, P. (2012). *Psychological Perspectives on Power and Domination: The Case of Adolf Hitler*. Routledge.

Montaigne, M. (1580). *Essays*. Penguin Classics.

Napoleon, B. (1861). *The Letters of Napoleon to Josephine*. H.S. Nichols.

Nietzsche, F. (1887). *On the Genealogy of Morality*. Cambridge University Press.

Plato. (4th century BC). *The Republic*. Oxford University Press.

Chapter 20: Gratitude

Tolle, E. (1997). *The Power of Now: A Guide to Spiritual Enlightenment.* New World Library.

Emmons, R. A. (2007). *Thanks!: How Practicing Gratitude Can Make You Happier.* Houghton Mifflin Harcourt.

Lyubomirsky, S. (2007). *The How of Happiness: A New Approach to Getting the Life You Want.* Penguin.

Seligman, M. E. P. (2002). *Authentic Happiness: Using the New Positive Psychology to Realize Your Potential for Lasting Fulfillment.* Free Press.

Wallace, D. F. (2005). *This Is Water: Some Thoughts, Delivered on a Significant Occasion, about Living a Compassionate Life.* Little, Brown.

Chapter 21: Refine

Carter, D. (2025). *Masculinity Reforged: Timeless Lessons for Modern Men.* [Author's original work].

Carnegie, A. (1889). *The Gospel of Wealth.* The North American Review.

Greene, R. (1998). *The 48 Laws of Power.* Viking Press.

Holiday, R. (2019). *Stillness Is the Key.* Portfolio.

Nietzsche, F. (1883). *Thus Spoke Zarathustra.* (W. Kaufmann, Trans.). Penguin Classics.

Seneca. (c. 65 AD). *Letters from a Stoic*. (R. Campbell, Trans.). Penguin Classics.

Tolle, E. (1997). *The Power of Now: A Guide to Spiritual Enlightenment*. New World Library.

Trivers, R. (1971). *The Evolution of Reciprocal Altruism*. The Quarterly Review of Biology, 46(1), 35-57.

Chapter 22: Reforged

Nietzsche, F. (1883-1885). *Thus spoke Zarathustra: A Book for All and None*. (T. Common, Trans.). Dover Publications.

Nietzsche, F. (1886). *Beyond Good and Evil: Prelude to a Philosophy of the Future*. (W. Kaufmann, Trans.). Vintage.

Nietzsche, F. (1887). *On the Genealogy of Morality: A Polemic*. (C. Diethe & K. Ansell-Pearson, Trans.). Cambridge University Press.

Kaufmann, W. (1974). *Nietzsche: Philosopher, Psychologist, Antichrist*. Princeton University Press.

Leiter, B. (2002). *Nietzsche on Morality*. Routledge.

Hales, S. D. (2000). *Nietzsche's Perspectivism*. University of Illinois Press.

World Health Organization. (2021). *Mental health Promotion Through Resilience and Self-mastery.* Retrieved from https://www.who.int.

Chapter 23: Legacy

Mandela, N. (1994). *Long Walk to Freedom: The Autobiography of Nelson Mandela.* Little, Brown and Company.

Carlin, J. (2008). *Playing the Enemy: Nelson Mandela and the Game that Made a Nation.* Penguin Books.

Sampson, A. (1999). *Mandela: The Authorized Biography.* HarperCollins.

Maxwell, J. C. (2008). *Leadership Gold: Lessons I've Learned From a Lifetime of Leading.* Thomas Nelson.

Brown, B. (2018). Dare to Lead: BraveWork. Tough Conversations. Whole Hearts. Random House.

Chapter 24: Honor

Benedict, R. (1946). *The Chrysanthemum and the Sword: Patterns of Japanese Culture.* Houghton Mifflin.

Cleary, T. (1999). *Code of the Samurai: A Modern Translation of the Bushido Shoshinshu of Taira Shigesuke.* Tuttle Publishing.

Plutarch. (75 A.D.). *Parallel Lives.* Harvard University Press.

Pressfield, S. (1998). *Gates of Fire: An Epic Novel of the Battle of Thermopylae*. Bantam Books.

Yamamoto, T. (1716). *Hagakure: The Secret Wisdom of the Samurai*. Kodansha International.

Conclusion

Dumas, A. (1844). *The Count of Monte Cristo*. Chapman & Hall.